CW01512118

ABOUT THE AUTHOR

Rachel Tsoumbakos has had several articles published through mainstream magazines and currently writes extensively for *The Inquisitr*. Over the years, Rachel has been interested in many aspects of history. When studying a Library Studies diploma, she discovered just how much she enjoyed researching and has since used these skills in several of her novels. However, it was her work with *The Inquisitr* that brought her into the world of the Vikings and she has spent several years delving into the sagas of this culture as well as the history of the Viking Age.

Rachel lives with her husband, two kids, three cats and flock of chickens in the idyllic Yarra Ranges located near Melbourne, Australia. When she isn't writing, she is working on her cardio as she trains for the zombie apocalypse.

FIND RACHEL ONLINE:

Facebook:
http://www.facebook.com/rtsoumbakos
Twitter:
http://twitter.com/#!/mrszoomby
Blog:
http://racheltsoumbakos.wordpress.com
Newsletter:
bit.ly/RachelNL

THE IRISH VIKING PRINCESS

RACHEL TSOUMBAKOS

THE IRISH VIKING PRINCESS

Rachel Tsoumbakos

Principle cover image: © Selenittt | DepositPhotos.com
Cover design: © Rachel Tsoumbakos
Time breaks designed using the Angerthas free font

unique electronic & print books

CONTENTS

Care eats the *heart* | if thou canst not *speak*
To another all thy *thought*.

~*Havamal*, from the *Poetic Edda*.

PROLOGUE

MELKORKA RUSHED TOWARDS THE FORT, HER heart knocking out a frenetic beat in her chest as she pumped her arms harder. She could see the Grianan of Aileach up ahead, its thick stone walls her only beacon of protection. Ever since she was young, she had been taught this was the only safe place against the raiding Finngaill.

These fierce warriors were all she ever heard about as her father discussed war with the other petty kings. From one length of their homeland to the other, Eriu appeared to have been invaded by the mighty and fearsome Norse. Melkorka was raised on their terror and now it seemed that it was finally her time to witness firsthand their brutality.

It was an event she had hoped would never arrive. Yet, here it was.

She looked at the red sky, fire lighting the night and closed her eyes briefly as she ran. All day she had been away, visiting her relatives at a nearby tuath. Her father had advised against it but she had gone against his wishes anyway.

And here she was now with no one to protect her.

Around her, Melkorka could hear the distant screams of the attack. The winds whipped in with the fearsome sounds, assaulting her. Clenching her jaw, she continued to run.

She would be safe once she reached the fort. The guards would see her coming and let her in. But she had to get there first.

The distance was closing between herself and the looming walls. The impressive feature was a dark hole against the fires burning around it. Melkorka wasn't sure if the Finngaill had lit those fires or if it was the work of her own people. She had never listened when talk turned to war so she had no idea of the strategies involved.

Her father, Myrkjartan, King of Aileach, had been aware of her own stupidity, and she now knew just how ridiculous she had been to ignore the ongoing talk of the continued raids. At least he had managed to instill in her the safety of the fort. So, now she ran as if she had a swath of Sluagh chasing her down.

Over the sounds of screams, there were also the brusque calls of men and the tormented shrieks of battle. Taking in the breadth of the landscape. Melkorka tried to work out where the sounds were coming from but the wind was also her enemy. It tore the sounds from one place and strew them through the air, depositing them in varied locations. Melkorka scraped her red hair out of her eyes, pulling it back behind her head. She hoped that by doing so it would help her hearing without it blanketing her ears.

It did not.

Melkorka continued to run as the burn in her chest continued, her ragged breaths slicing at her raw throat. It was only then that she realised she had been screaming as she ran. The hollow sound was a dull echo now, letting her know that she had been doing it for a long time. She tried to swallow the noise back, her gaze darting around. Melkorka didn't want to be the beacon that alerted the Finngaill to her presence.

Still, she screamed. There was no way her own body was going to let up. It was a traitor that she couldn't escape from.

She had no choice but to try and outrun anyone that approached. Melkorka brought her arms in closer, hunching over, attempting to draw more speed out of her tiring gait.

The walls were blocking out the sight of the flames and the moon was obstructed from her sight, making it even harder to see her surrounds.

That had to be a good sign.

She was so close that she felt like she could reach out and touch the wall as it towered over her. Yet, she continued to run, knowing that her sense of perception was distorted upon approach.

Gazing higher, she tried to find the guards who she knew were there and on high alert, ready to let people in who needed shelter. In her frantic haste, though, she couldn't see anything, only the dark of night.

"Hello!" she called hoarsely. Her voice was feeble, quiet in comparison to the frenetic noises of terror surrounding her.

She realised too late that she should never have run to the Grianan of Aileach for protection.

Instead, she should have stayed where she was, out in the forest surrounding the fort. Melkorka didn't know the woods here as well as her own homeland but she knew the best places to hide regardless of location. There were always old logs to be found or a protective thicket that she could fight her way into the middle of in order to be overlooked by the Finngaill. It would have been much safer than where she was at present.

Melkorka considered turning, of running back the way in which she had come. Even as she turned, she knew that it was too late.

Strong arms reached around her, lifting her high and throwing her over their shoulder. She smelled the hideous musk of sweat and blood and carnage emanating off the raider's body.

Melkorka struggled. Her fists knotted up and she pummelled the man's back. He laughed at her before slapping her behind and striding off.

Speaking in a language that she barely understood, another man appeared and grabbed at her. She was quickly exchanged between the two and the new man smelled worse than the first.

This time she gouged her fingernails into the man's back, trying to make him bleed. Once again, her feeble attempts were laughed at as he walked towards one of the huge fires burning.

Melkorka paused only briefly in her onslaught as she sighted a looming cage. Inside were a variety of people. All looks scared and she swallowed hard at her destiny.

She was a princess of Eriu, not a slave. There was no way that she wanted this to be her new reality.

However, as the door was opened and shriek of metal greeted her, she knew that her life was about to change. The gaping maw of the cage reached out for her and it was all that she could see.

The vast opening consumed her even before the man abruptly yanked her down off his shoulder and threw inside the cage. Melkorka landed haphazardly on top of the warmth of other bodies. She heard grunts and yelps as she collided with people. Her instincts saw her apologising for the injuries, for inflicting more accidental pain on others. She was a princess, after all, and manners had been ingrained in her since birth.

Yet, she knew that none of that mattered anymore.

As the gate closed, silenced after only the clang of metal against metal, she knew that her life was now forfeit, that her upbringing meant nothing and that her very survival was to be an ongoing struggle.

It was a battle that she didn't even know if she wanted to fight.

Perhaps, she should act up, cause such a ruckus that her captors would see fit to have her killed rather than to sell her into slavery.

Oh yes, while she may have ignored all of her father's talk of war strategy, her mother had made sure to instill a reasonable fear regarding what happened to pretty young women who were caught up in the spoils of war.

Melkorka did not want to be a slave or a man's property. There was no way that she wanted to end up sold to another person, of having to live under someone else's rule, under their command and continued control.

Melkorka would rather die than have that happen to her.

Then, the sound of crying broke into her thoughts and she turned.

In the corner of the cage, illuminated by the fire, was a terrified young girl. Melkorka had no idea of who she was but she reached over and took the girl's hand. Their fingers entwined and she felt the fear of what she was about to do.

She felt the fear of living.

CHAPTER 1: MELKORKA

"MY NAME IS GILLI," THE MAN SAID IN Melkorka's native tongue.

His accent was heavy and the words cut in and out but she understood him well enough. Even though she was raised in a high-status family, a king's work often saw peasants visiting, requesting extensions and offering gifts as well as disputing squabbles over their day-to-day living. So, she had heard many varied accents before now. Even though Gilli's accent was completely foreign to her, she could still work out the machinations of it. In fact, she could even understand some of the language of the Norse thanks to those who had given up raiding and settled as merchants. Because of this, she knew enough to understand that this man was not one of the Finngaill.

Melkorka wondered just how far he had come from and wished bitterly that he had never left his country of origin, that he had never decided that slave-taking was a good idea for a living. As if that would somehow change her outcome, that she would never have wound up in this position except for the decision of a single man.

Still, on some level, Melkorka knew that slaves were necessary to smooth the way for everyone else. Even she used them regularly. She thought of her nanny, the sweet old woman who had birthed and raised her. Ina was an owned woman, even if Melkorka had never really thought of her as such. There were others, too. Slaves helped with her dressing, bathing, and with her disrobing at the end of every day.

To be on the reverse end of these procedures terrified her. She had no idea how to do any of these tasks, nor did she have the inclinations to try.

Of course, there was another option. Melkorka shuddered at the thought.

She could be sold as a concubine. Sex was not a mystery to her as she had seen enough of it in her day-to-day living, and it was never hidden away like it was rumoured to be with those of the strange Christian faith. However, she was still terrified of being forced into the occupation. She had only just come into an age where she could be married, after all.

Gritting her teeth against the equally unappealing options, she glanced across the line of women until her gaze landed on Roisin, the young girl that she had bonded with ever since their first night of captivity at the fort. She would have it even harder if she was selected as a concubine. The child was only ten years of age and her eyes rounded with fear as Gilli spoke of what was to become of them all.

Melkorka waited patiently, her gaze never leaving the frightened child until the girl's gaze flitted in her direction. As soon as they made eye contact, Melkorka smiled. It was a brief occurrence. Her lips felt like they would crack if she tried any harder as her outward expression battled with how she felt on the inside. Yet, it seemed to be enough. She watched as Roisin attempted a smile back at her and then took a deep breath, as though to calm herself.

"We will be travelling to Norway soon, where I will be able to fetch the best price for all of you. If any of you can speak the language, let me know ahead of time. We will attempt to teach you as we travel. Otherwise, I will sell you dependent on requirement."

Melkorka's stomach dropped. She only knew enough of the language in order to buy wares from her local marketplace. Being able to speak the foreign tongue would make her more valuable and much more likely to be selected for a higher position rather than that of the lowliest of slaves or concubines.

Swallowing hard, she waited while another Finngaill stepped up and led them all away. They were tied together with rope and it chafed at her wrists. Already, she was bleeding in one spot and the movement was excruciating as the man yanked at the lead.

Initially, when they had started to travel, no one thought to allow them to stop for toileting or the such and had arrived in such a state that even the Finngaill turned their noses up at them.

They had forced them all into the river after that, their hands tied for the first time. Not even stripping them down, they shivered afterward as their damp clothing stuck to their bodies. Once again, no one had offered to allow them to stand by the fire to dry off. Instead, they had been pushed into a makeshift hut and they had to huddle together in order to stay warm.

Each day after that they travelled. And, every night they were thrown into a hut. It was a better life than the first leg of their journey but, only just. Nighttime was the only time that they could be free of captivity and to move around more freely, even if guards kept a vigilant stand outside. Already, the women knew of each other, had learned their names and the details of their previous lives.

Many of them told a similar story. Some were captured while they slept, some raped in the process, others ran down in a field like Melkorka. Still, it was all the same. They were slaves now and the only friends in the world they had were the women surrounding them. It was a delicate balance, however.

"Gilli," said Onora. "I speak some Norse. Perhaps I could be of use to you?"

The woman purred the words, leaning forward and smiling at Gilli. Melkorka rolled her eyes and Roisin smirked at her response.

"Of course, my dear," the man replied. "Might I suggest then that you start to teach the others since you are proficient in both languages."

Onora scowled when Gilli turned his back, her smile returning as soon as the man had scoped the line of women and returned his gaze in her direction.

"I will teach it if I have to. However, there are women here that have been mean to me and I would not want to help them if I have to."

Melkorka watched Onora, already wise to her tricks. While some of the women were still scared of the Finngaill others, like Onora, were using their female wiles to their advantage to gain some leverage or favour within their new life.

Melkorka could understand why the women were doing this. Still, she didn't like it. Nor did she trust the women at all.

"Like who?" Gilli asked, raising an eyebrow. Melkorka supposed the merchant had already seen this behaviour before. Still, he seemed to allow it.

"Some, like Failenn, have been critical of me for alerting you to Uallach's plan to escape. Since then, the women have been relentless in harassing me."

Glancing to Failenn, Melkorka could see the woman's face grow red with anger. However, after what had happened to Uallach, few would speak up in defense of themselves.

Uallach was now kept separate from them at night. They all suspected that the Finngaill used her badly, not only from the bruises that now appeared on her face but from the way that the poor woman huddled down low and never made eye contact with anyone else.

Melkorka may want to escape, may even try it if the opportunity arose but she would not speak of it, not even to Roisin for fear that even the child would turn against her in to better her own position.

"What happened to Uallach should be a lesson to you all that you need to do as you are told," Gilli said. He directed his gaze at Onora before speaking further. "I would like you to help the other women. Otherwise, you might end up alongside the very woman you spoke out about."

She shouldn't smile but Melkorka couldn't help it as Onora's hands clenched up into fists and she tried to control herself. Even this woman was fearful of the consequences of the guards and it gave Melkorka some comfort knowing that there was protection for those who abided by the laws of the trader, little that it may be.

As the women were led back towards their hut, Gilli walked up to the man leading them and whispered something to him. Melkorka strained against the noise of her surrounds and tried in vain to hear what was being said. Gilli spoke in his native tongue, though, Melkorka eventually realised and slackened her posture, already giving up on the words.

"You, and you," Gilli was now saying, pointing his grubby finger towards two of the women at the front of the line.

Melkorka watched as they continued to look over the group. As her gaze followed the men, she could see Onora standing taller. Even after being told off, the woman still tried her hardest to be noticed by the guards in an effort to get special favours. However, Gilli passed over the woman and continued to search the group before settling on another.

"And you."

Melkorka was not sure what to make of it. Then, Gilli's stubby finger thrust towards her.

"This one too," he said before turning back to the guard. "She looks important as well. They should all fetch a good price, even if they do not speak the language."

Gilli turned then, leaving the group as another guard helped the first one undo the ropes binding them all. Melkorka searched frantically for Roisin and saw that fear was back on the child's face. Roisin was not one of those selected and, regardless of their fates, it seemed likely that they would never see each other again because of Gilli's actions.

Melkorka tried to smile once more but her face was stone and would not conform to her wishes. Roisin's eyes widened in response and Melkorka watched as tears started to form in the young girl's eyes. Her heart broke with the horror of it all and she wished, once again, that she had made different choices on the day of her abduction.

Even after everything that Gilli had just said about them being able to better themselves, it all came down to what they looked like and whether the trader thought the women would gain more coin because of it. The notion made Melkorka feel ill.

One man reached her and Melkorka closed her eyes as her own tears threatened. She would not show her emotion to the Finngaill. Not her fear and desolation, at least.

Roughly, her hands were pulled from the harsh rope and Melkorka bit the inside of her cheek rather than squawk out in pain. Another guard grabbed her arm, his fingers pinching into her soft skin.

The man looked at her, pulling her sleeve up as he did so before muttering something in a different language. He pointed at her gold armband, so she knew what was coming next and she could no longer help it as the threatening tears started to fall.

This band was her last remaining connection to her old life and to her family. Her father had presented it to her as a gift when she was born and it wasn't that long ago that she was old enough for the band to fill her properly. She did not want to give it up.

"Leave it," Gilli said and Melkorka opened her eyes, surprised that he spoke in her language to the guard. "It will help to prove her worth."

She staggered against the news and the guard pulled more roughly at her in response. Snapping herself upright, Melkorka allowed the man to lead her away from the other women. She turned back and the group watched her being led away. Singling in on Roisin, her tears continued to fall.

CHAPTER 2: MELKORKA

THE SMELL OF SICKNESS WAS STRONG TODAY. The sea had been alive with the storm this morning and everyone was suffering because of it. Well, maybe not the Finngaill. They seemed immune to everything but the sharp end of a sword.

Melkorka herself had lost count of the times that she had to lean overboard and lose the contents of her stomach. She had barely eaten over the last few days and her vision swam with dark spots because of this. Already, two women had died and their lifeless forms had been thrown overboard.

The men laughed as they disposed of the women and it made Melkorka feel even sicker that no one cared for them, for these creatures who had previous lives, with loved ones still at home mourning their captivity. Now, their families would never know how they had died or even that they had died at all.

Melkorka was sad with that knowledge. Would anyone wonder about her fate at home? Her father would worry, for certain, and her sisters would likely fret. Her mother was long dead and Melkorka hoped that she thought of her in the afterlife. A vision of her nanny flashed across her mind and of how she had always fussed over her. Ina would remember her, as well.

Still, it wasn't enough. Knowing that her family cared, that they were concerned about what had happened to her was not enough for her to maintain a will to live during the wretched journey.

Gazing at the sky, in a brief moment of misery, Melkorka begged the gods to let her die. Living was too hard, or it would be now that she was captured and taken as a slave. Her insides clenched and her fingers fisted together, her fingernails cutting painfully into her palms. The pain brought an edge to her emotions, engulfing her, owning her in her desolation. Looking across the water, Melkorka wondered what it would feel like to drop into the water and to sink to the very bottom.

"Back you come," one of the Finngaill said as if knowing her very thoughts.

Shuddering, Melkorka leaned back, her fingers wrapping around a post and she leaned into it, suddenly exhausted by her fate. Glancing around, she focused in on the others who shared her journey. The boat that she was travelling on housed a great many women who were all crammed together in a single section. They all shared the same misery as her and that, somehow, was a comfort to her in the moment.

If they could keep breathing in and out, if they could continue to get up every morning and live, then so could she. She tried to remember Roisin's face but found that the child's face swam out of her memory now, a shadow of a figure that she could barely remember.

At least the sweet child was not with them. Melkorka couldn't stand it if Roisin were to be sold as a concubine as she would be.

Gilli had explained it so when they set sail and Melkorka had no idea how she felt about that. She was somewhat relieved at not having to perform the rote meaningless tasks as that of a handmaiden and of becoming a forgotten woman, lost to the background of the much richer lives of those she would serve. And, she was definitely thankful that it meant that she would not become a farmhand, destined to sleep with the animals and tend to their messy undertakings.

Still, a concubine held its own dangers.

She would be a possession to a man—any man—and she had no choice over him. That was what scared her the most. Melkorka could get used to being used. It was just sex, after all. But any man could purchase her. An old man, or one with strange growths on his body, or one that smelled bad.

However, what she was most fearful of was how he could treat her. She might be bought by someone cruel, one who mistreated her or used her badly. Every time she thought of being abused in that manner, her breath quickened and her heart raced in fear.

Melkorka could stand being sold to a kind man, even if he was ugly or old. If he treated her well, even as a second wife, she could somehow accept her fate. However, if the man was mean and beat her, or shared her with anyone, she could not stomach that.

She was a princess and, still, she held strong to the notion of being treated as such. Even in this wretched situation, she hoped her worth would be realised. Melkorka also knew that this hope was a ridiculous fantasy that would likely never come true. Even as she lurched overboard to vomit once more, she laughed at her own stupidity.

"You, this way," the guard who had pulled her back a moment earlier said as he grabbed her arm.

His foreign language was already making sense to her. She had studied the men hard during the journey. Always remaining silent in order to hear their words, to make sense of what they were saying and comparing them to the ones that Gilli used in her own tongue. She was thankful at being able to pick up the language so quickly.

The guards suspected she was dumb through her lack of speech. This knowledge was something that she had picked up not long after she started trying to learn their language. It wasn't that she couldn't talk, she had done plenty of that with the women early on before the likes of Onora had shown her true worth. Instead, it was just that she felt like she had nothing to say to these vile men and that her time could be better spent learning their language. That sort of knowledge was power, after all. And, while they were making wild assumptions about Melkorka, they were also underestimating her and that was always something that could be used to a woman's advantage.

Melkorka wiped her hand across her mouth and wished that she had time to grab a sip of water. However, she knew already that their guards were not patient and did not wait while you finished your task or made a request. No, he would use his hand on her and she would receive another bruise if she reached for a drink. Instead, Melkorka lowered her head and followed the man as he laughed at her.

"Dumb mute," he commented before striding away.

It was a name they used often on her but she didn't care. Melkorka had nothing of importance to say to them anyway. They were not interested in what she had to say so why should she speak?

Gritting her teeth, she vowed not to speak again while in captivity. Not to the Finngaill, at least. Through the grim situation, the thought made her smile. Her lack of speech was the only thing she could control now. It was stupid to be proud of it. Yet, in the horrible world in which she now lived it was also a comfort to know that she could control some part of her destiny. Gilli may consider her to be of high standing but she would do everything within her control to make it hard to sell her off.

CHAPTER 3: HOSKULD

HOSKULD ALWAYS ENJOYED THESE TRIPS away from home. To travel the world and to see faraway places was what he yearned for. It was in his blood and he relished the prospect of the trip, hungered for it while he was at home in Iceland.

It wasn't that he didn't like where he lived, he did. Even as he set foot on Norwegian soil, he still wished for the open vistas and volcanic mountains back home. Norway was stunning with its waterfalls and fjords and the green slopes filled with evergreens. However, it felt closed in to him. He could only see as far as the mountains allowed. In the Laxardal region of Iceland, he could see as far as his eyes would allow. The plains stretching out and offering a plethora of possibilities.

No, the reason he enjoyed these trips so much was because it gave him time away from his wife, Jorunn. And, after the argument he'd had prior to his departure, this trip was especially welcomed.

"It's good to see you again," Hrut said and Hoskuld turned and embraced his half-brother.

"And you, too," Hoskuld replied as he sized Hrut up. "How have you grown even taller since our last meeting?"

"It is the air over here," he replied. "Or so my mother says. Honestly, I think it has more to do with the hard training I am under with the king."

Hoskuld nodded. Hrut was a part of King Haakon's guard. It was a prestige position that Hoskuld himself had helped the lad to secure.

"I must make myself known to the king during this trip," he said as he walked alongside Hrut. "It has been a while since we have conversed and I am sure that Haakon is wondering if I still count myself among his men."

"Indeed, he is. But first, come and drink with me. Groa is already here."

"I haven't seen her for the longest time! Is she still married to Veleiv?"

"Aye, she is," Hrut replied as he pushed open the door to a longhouse.

Stepping inside the noise swelled over him and Hoskuld waited as his eyes adjusted. There was light in here but the midday sun was stronger so he only noticed his sister in the moment before she leaped at him.

"Hoskuld!" she exclaimed.

"It has been a while, hasn't it?" he returned as he spun Groa around.

"Too long. But you've finally made it. Here, sit with us. There is bread and ale already set."

Hoskuld followed her towards the back of the long hall. He was jostled between people, some of which were already drunk and Hoskuld smiled at them as he passed. He was thankful to fall into a seat, though, and grabbed at the ale and food on offer.

Taking a bite of the bread, Hoskuld sighed into his food. "This is so much better than ship's biscuits and smoked herrings."

The ale was good too, sweet and not at all resembling the vinegar he had been drinking on the voyage. Yes, it was good to be on solid soil once more.

"How are things back at home?" Groa asked, shouting over the noise of the room. Everywhere, people were talking, laughing, even singing, and Hoskuld welcomed the merriment. As Veleiv sat down next to Groa, he clapped a hand on Hoskuld's shoulder and Hoskuld nodded in reply.

"Everything is good," he replied, avoiding what he knew his sister was really asking about. "We had a decent crop haul last year so I have no fear of travelling. My family is well provided for because of this."

"How is Jorunn?"

Groa said his wife's name slowly, sly with her tone and Hoskuld could not avoid answering any longer.

"She is the same as she always is."

Hrut nudged his elbow into Hoskuld's ribs. "Perhaps you can find someone more accommodating while you are here?"

"Jorunn is a great wife," Hoskuld countered but the words were hollow.

The group laughed at him even as he took another sip of ale and tried to smile through his false words. There was no convincing his family that his marriage was happy or passionate.

There was a great difference between being a great wife and a great friend. And, to be honest, Jorunn was neither.

Although, his sense of honour forced him to lie in front of his family. He and Jorunn may not be the best-matched couple but she had never given him a reason to cast her aside so he supposed it could be worse than what it was. Although, the bitterness in her words at his departure still played across his mind and he wondered if she really did still wait for him at home.

"Oh, Hoskuld," Groa said as she patted him on the arm. "You are not a great liar. There is no shame in your marriage but you deserve more. You should have what Veleiv and I do."

She leaned over and kissed her husband and Hoskuld had to look away. He couldn't remember the last time he had shown open affection to Jorunn in a public place. Even with the massive age difference between his sister and Veleiv, they still managed to find more passion in this one moment than Hoskuld and his wife had in their entire marriage.

In fact, he couldn't remember the last time either of them showed affection towards the other. Jorunn kept their home and family happy and tended to everything well but she ignored him and what he really needed.

He would never say it out loud. He was even embarrassed to think it but what he really wanted was a woman who was excited to see him, who could share his bed and tend to his needs rather than everyone else's. Instead, what he had was a woman who called him a fool and hoped that his voyage was complicated by bad weather. Although, he understood the darker meaning well.

As he gazed at his sister still wrapped in her husband's arms, he wished that a woman would behave with him as Groa did around Veleiv.

Yes, maybe he would keep an eye out for someone who

could help him out in that manner.

"Try Gilli the Russian," Veleiv said. "He sells the best concubines."

Hoskuld nodded in response but said nothing. Despite their harsh words before he left, he did usually get along well with Jorunn and he didn't really want to admit just how loveless their marriage was now.

"Tell me more about working under King Haakon," Hoskuld said, turning to Hrut and wanting to forget his life back home.

"He is a good king, and lucky with his long reign, but you know that already," Hrut said before swallowing back the remainder of his ale. A serving woman was immediately at his side, topping his glass up and Hrut winked at her. As she turned to leave, he slapped her on the arse and the maid giggled in reply.

"I need to see the king regarding new timber for my home but maybe I should stay longer than that?"

"Of course, I am sure Haakon would like that."

"And, what of Denmark?" Hoskuld asked, turning to his sister once more. "Is it still as beautiful as you keep insisting?"

Hoskuld has long suspected that Groa was homesick but continued to perpetuate the idea that she loved her new home country. In the way in which Hoskuld danced around his loveless marriage, so too did Groa avoid the fact that she was not entirely happy in Denmark.

"It is glorious," she replied, smiling at her husband. "You still haven't visited me, though. I think you would love it. It is so different from home. How do you even stand it there?"

"How can you not love Iceland?" Hoskuld replied. "It is better than any place in the world. I could never leave it permanently."

And, he was telling the truth. His home was where his heart was. He loved the Laxardal region more than his wife, which was an easy task. No, the land he grew up in was under his skin. It was a part of him and he could never imagine calling another place home.

"Iceland is nothing but a place in which to be born and leave," Groa scoffed at him.

He frowned. "I disagree, and I think you do too. Surely you still hunger for home, for the history of the place, the memories, and the unbroken line that our family has there?"

Groa looked downwards, avoiding his gaze. She tore off a piece of bread and washed it down with her ale rather than look at him. He had hit a soft spot, perhaps even intentionally.

Reaching over, he clasped her hand. "I am sorry," he whispered and she finally looked back at him.

"At least I am happy in my marriage and am not living in the past," she replied and Hoskuld had nothing to say to that.

CHAPTER 4: HOSKULD

THE TENT WAS IMPRESSIVE EVEN IF IT WAS pushed all the way back from the centre of activity. Hoskuld swallowed hard before scratching at the door. He was not even sure he should be doing this.

Jorunn would be mad, even though it was socially acceptable for him to have a concubine. She liked control and this was not something which she could command. But he was still resentful because of her harsh words towards him and this felt like the perfect way in which to retaliate.

Once he bought a woman and took her home, she would be stuck with the decision. Perhaps, it would make her regret how she had spoken to him, belittling him in front of their children. Normally, Jorunn never spoke harshly of him in front of their offspring. However, this time she had been so mad that the words were out of her mouth before she could control them. And, once she had started, there was no stopping.

A door opened, pulling Hoskuld from his musings. Smiling at the man, he followed him inside the establishment.

Wares lined the walls and were covering tables. Everywhere Hoskuld looked there were all assortments of strange finery. Gilli was reputed to be one of the best traders at the meeting. In fact, he was considered the best merchant of all and his wealth was beyond compare for his kind because of it.

Hoskuld was distracted by the shine of fine metalwork and the strange objects from faraway places. He reached out and touched some linen that was patterned with unusual markings and wondered where it had come from. Then, his attention was drawn to a tightly woven basket containing some sort of aromatic spice. There was so much to see, so much to distract him. Yet, he pulled away, ignoring all of it and turned back to Gilli the Russian.

"I hear that you sell thralls."

"Of course," the man replied in a thick accent. "Follow me."

Hoskuld was led through the tent and towards the back where another curtain was quickly pulled aside. The soft hum of female voices stopped as soon as Gilli opened the door and Hoskuld was presented with twelve frightened faces.

For a moment, as he gazed upon the wide eyes and trembling lips, Hoskuld regretted his decision. These women look terrified and not at all conducive to the sort of concubine he was looking for.

Even still, one woman caught his attention. At the end of the line sat a female whose face was downturned, as if she had no interest in any of the goings-on around her. Her red hair fanned out over her shoulders and Hoskuld had never seen anything like it. Sure, there were redheads among his community but her fiery hair seemed to circle her face and draw attention to her beauty.

Her delicate skin glowed, also drawing him in with the captivating beauty of this fine creature. "How much for the one on the end?"

The woman looked up at his words and he knew that he understood her. It was an advantage to have her already speak his language and he smiled tentatively at her. She scowled in response.

"This one is very expensive," Gilli replied. "I will take no less than three marks of silver for her. Are you sure you would not like one of the others?"

"Why is she so much better than the others?" Hoskuld asked. Although, he already knew that whatever Gilli said would not sway him. This woman was an exquisite creature, so fair, so breathtakingly beautiful that he felt he had no choice but to own her.

"She is of royal blood," Gilli replied and Hoskuld tried not to snort.

It was the usual scheme. There was always one in the batch—usually the one you had just shown an interest in and was keen to purchase—that suddenly belonged to royal stock.

Hoskuld cocked his head at the woman and tried to see her without the ragged clothing. Yes, she was beautiful but that didn't automatically give her a higher pedigree. In fact, some of the ugliest women he had ever met were princesses and queens.

However, this one held herself tall, her neck long and elegant. Her shoulders were defiantly squared, like she knew that she was more important than the others in the room.

Gilli's words might just be true, Hoskuld thought. Although, he had also heard of conniving merchants who collaborated with their slaves and taught them how they should put on airs and graces in order to behave like a woman of luxury.

He looked back at Gilli.

"I don't believe you," he said, although he actually did. "She looks like common stock to me."

Gilli shrugged and turned away, one hand reaching out to point at the other women. "Then pick another. They are all one mark of silver and ready for the taking."

Hoskuld took another look along the line. There were certainly some beautiful women in the batch. All of the women wore stunning gowns, their hair was brushed and they appeared to be in fine health.

He tried to select another, to choose one that was cheaper. It wasn't that he didn't have the money but, rather, that he wanted his money's worth. While the redhead was stunning, she appeared more reserved than the others. He didn't want to spend his funds only to discover that he had bought himself another woman just like his wife.

Yet, she was also the only one who hadn't looked fearful when he entered. He thought of Jorunn and of how much she didn't want him. These women were the same. The redhead, on the other hand, was defiant, different.

He couldn't focus on any other woman. There was no pull to any of them, no attraction like he had instantly felt with the redhead. He went to stand in front of her once more.

"She is also a mute," Gilli said. "The woman may be of royal stock but you will not get a word out of her. She seems able to perform tasks though, so she may not be stupid as well."

"Then it is doubly strange that you are selling her off at such a high price. Perhaps you are trying to cheat me."

"How can I be doing that if I am laying all the facts down in front of you? I have not been deceptive regarding her faults. Once again, feel free to pick another, or be done with wasting my time."

Hoskuld leaned in, really scrutinizing the woman. "I am not wasting your time, I will be walking out of here with a concubine, regardless of which one. Tell me, where was she taken from?"

"She came from Eriu during an attack by the Rus. I was lucky to secure her before her purity was taken."

Hoskuld assumed Gilli was talking more lies. Not that it mattered to him whether he was her first. He was not like the Christians who made strange laws regarding when a woman could partake in pleasure.

"I care not for her purity," Hoskuld replied with a wave of his hand. "In fact, I care not for her lineage either."

He had already decided that he would pay whatever it took for the fine woman. He had seen the fine armband she wore. It was not of Rus workings, nor was it Icelandic. No, he was convinced that it was hers from before her abduction. It was high quality so he knew that, even if she was not a princess, her family could afford such niceties.

"I will take her," Hoskuld continued before standing up. "I will pay your three marks of silver as well."

Reaching for his coin bag, Hoskuld shook it as he pulled it from his waist tie. Gilli pulled out a scale and they promptly measured out the correct amount.

"It is good doing business with you," Gilli said as he grabbed the seated woman and pulled her to a standing position. "Please, come again. After all, you can never have too many concubines."

Gilli laughed at his own comment but Hoskuld was not interested. Instead, he nodded at the man and took the woman's hand, leading her from the hut and out into the bright daylight. He watched as she squinted, trying to adjust to the glaring day.

"How long has it been since you were outside?" he asked and the woman ignored him. Perhaps Gilli had not lied about her being a mute after all.

He smiled at her when she focused on him. She frowned her reply but it was a subtle action as if she were hiding her true feelings. The woman had likely been beaten for less and Hoskuld suddenly felt a swell of emotion. He wanted to protect this glorious creature, to shelter her from any more pain. It washed over him, confusing him but also a comfort as he realised that this woman standing in front of him might be his only chance in which to find happiness.

"I won't hurt you," he finally said as he looked deep into her eyes. "I will give you time to adjust."

If he wasn't mistaken, the woman ducked her head just slightly, as if acknowledging his words. Hoskuld felt his heart swell even further.

CHAPTER 5: MELKORKA

AS SOON AS THE MAN HAD WALKED INTO THE hut, Melkorka knew her life was about to change. She could feel it in her bones in the way she felt the stirrings of spring and when someone was lying to her father about not being able to meet their tithe. Her nanny had called it a gift but it didn't feel like one now.

The air had rushed into the room, cool and crisp and smelling of new beginnings. She waited patiently, being good at that now. The more that she refrained from speaking, the more people closed up around her and didn't share information. Even the women in the room with her no longer talked to her. Melkorka could feel herself shutting up permanently, as if she could cocoon herself away and the outside world could not affect her because of it.

Gilli had brought the man through the curtain and she smelled the musky aroma of him. There was always the layer of sweat and dirt but, underneath that was the scent of his true being. Before Melkorka glanced up at him, her eyes quick and her gaze unnoticed by others, she knew that she would be chosen by him.

He was tall, just like his kind seemed to be. All of the Finngaill that she had come across were enormous, broad and wild. They had to be so that they could instill the fear that they did in others. But their strength was legendary as well and that probably accounted for some of their girth.

This man was no exception. His hair had been tamed at one point with a layer of braids. However, his mane, the colour of straw at the end of summer, had managed to wriggle free over time and tangled together creating matts that sprung out in all directions. His beard was braided in places, beaded in others and they jangled as he entered the room.

She felt the warmth of his breath as he leaned over the group and made his selection. Every time his blue-eyed gaze landed on her she swore she could feel it even though she didn't risk sighting him in order to confirm it. Her skin tingled in anticipation. Melkorka fought the urge to glace his way once more, to see him close up and to confirm that he was as handsome as she first suspected.

When he spoke to Gilli, his voice was gruff, hurried, like he didn't have time for the merchant's stories. While Gilli may be telling the truth about her lineage, Melkorka knew that he was only guessing. She had told no one of who her father was for fear that they might try to extort money out of him by way of a ransom. Of course, they likely didn't care one bit about her being a princess. After all, warm bodies sold regardless of whether or not a princess was purchased.

Knowing who she was, along with the knowledge that others didn't gave her a sense of power. It was all that she had left. That and the armband her father gave her. Instinctively, she rubbed at it as the man made his final deal with Gilli and then again as he reached out and took her arm and led her away from Gilli's tent.

She didn't miss the tent or the women that she had been bunched together with. No, what she missed was her homeland, her people, the everyday normalness that she had grown up with. The sun assaulted her as they stepped through the doorway and she squinted against it, trying to see her surrounds.

As her eyes adjusted, she looked around discreetly. Melkorka was still scared, worried that the man who bought her would be cruel, even if she hadn't sensed that as he spoke. Instead, he had seemed kind, or at least more so than she had ever been told the Finngaill could be.

Speaking to her gently, he explained where they were going. He had a tent on the other side of the gathering and they had to walk through the entire marketplace. The sounds overwhelmed her and she was thankful that his hand circled her arm, holding her up against the onslaught.

Even still, Melkorka wanted to run. Partly because she wanted to escape, although she had no idea where she would go in this foreign land. But, another part of her wanted to dart away merely to get through the encampment, to find a quiet place so that she could be alone and adjust to her position. In all the time that she had been in captivity, she had scarcely found a moment to be by herself. And, that was what she needed more than anything else.

She was naturally a loner; her father had chided her for it and it was what had managed to get her kidnapped. If only she hadn't decided to wander through the woods. She had told him she was visiting, and she had spent time with people. However, the main reason she left that day was so that she could be alone. If only she had stayed in the village as her father wanted, then she would still be there now.

Or, perhaps she would be dead. Melkorka wondered about that, about whether or not her family still lived. Maybe her father was dead. She hadn't contemplated that before and the thought made her choke on her emotions. She staggered and the man's hand tightened around her arm.

"Are you alright?" he asked and Melkorka turned towards him, finally risking looking fully at him.

His crisp blue eyes, the colour of the sky in summer, gazed at her and she fought the urge to shiver in response. She wanted to talk to him, to tell him, in his own tongue, that she would be fine, that she just needed a moment to herself so that she could make sense of everything that had happened to her. But she couldn't say a word. She couldn't even move her lips or open her mouth in response, so all she did was to dip her head in response.

The man grunted back at her and they continued through the crowd. Melkorka tried not to look around after that. There were too many faces, too many strange people for her to fully comprehend.

𝕄

THE ROOM WAS FILLED with people and Melkorka wanted to close her eyes, close her ears, close her very mind against it all. The noise rose as new people arrived and she couldn't believe that so many people could cram themselves into the space.

As they moved through the crowd, there were slight touches, a hand at her chest, another squeezing her behind. With the mass of people, she assumed that they were accidental touches. However, after having to pull her hand away quickly from a man's crotch after he leered at her and laughed, she felt like perhaps they were not and this room was just a collection of depravity.

Always, though, there was a hand at her back belonging to her new owner. She was apprehensive about what would come next. The women had always whispered about owners and the obligations involved with being a slave. Melkorka had always tried not to think about it but now there was nothing else but the concept. She swallowed hard as she thought about what she would have to do tonight when they lay down in his bed. Melkorka flinched as images rose to her mind. They were all make-believe since she had never laid with anyone before.

Although, there was that one time when she canoodled with that man as the Beltane fire roared behind them. She had been drunk on ale and he was a stranger passing through.

Their embrace had been wonderful and his hands wandering her body were just as delightful. Melkorka shivered with the thought and the brush of the new man's hand against her back summoned the pull she had felt on that summer's night.

Perhaps this man would want to do that too, to kiss her neck and to run his hands over the swell of her breasts. While she liked the idea of being touched by someone again as the fire of desire rose quickly in her, she abhorred the circumstances under which it would occur. Plus, the Finngaill were known for their rough ways and for forcing themselves on women.

Melkorka stole another glance at the man. He was taking a cup of ale from a serving woman and she took a good look at her too. This would likely be her life now. Even as a concubine, there would be tasks she would need to learn. She should understand just how to hand out ale and food and whatever it was that this man would call for over her lifetime. Her lifetime. She sighed at the thought as the true reality of it fell on her.

She would never marry a prince, never have children who would be grandsires of the king. Nor would she converse with her sisters or see her family at all. Instead, she would spend her life here and she would have to be ready for his every whim and fancy.

A sob choked out and she was thankful that the room was so noisy. Melkorka wanted to let her hot tears fall but she fought bitterly against it, against the public display of her own misery. No, she would wait until she was alone, whenever that would likely be, and cry on her own time, without the prying eyes of others. Her tears, along with her words, would be her own treats and not for anyone else.

"Here's some ale," the man said and he thrust the cup into her hand. Melkorka drank it down quickly, only realising how thirsty she was when the drink was presented. Her stomach responded as well. "My, aren't you thirsty then. How about some food?"

Melkorka looked at the man, searched his face. He was younger than she thought. His scraggly hair and looming form made her think that he was much older than herself. Now, she saw that his skin was smooth in between the slices of battle wounds. He was certainly older than her but not as old as her father, which was her first impression. Not that it made any difference. He would likely bed her regardless of either of their ages.

"Food?" he prompted once more. He looked concerned as he mimicked the act of eating, as though he didn't believe that she understood his words, that she was stupid as well as silent.

Melkorka nodded her head and the man smiled broadly. His face lit up and his eyes danced as he did so and Melkorka was tempted to join in his mirth. Instead, she remained quiet, her face stony and she watched as the man's smile drooped. He turned, his thick arm reaching up to draw attention to himself and a maiden with a tray of food made her way through the crowd towards him.

She stared at the food when it was presented to her. The man had moved them off to one side and, somehow, they had actually ended up on one of the benches that ran the length of the room. Next to them was a small table, barely more than a shelf, and Melkorka put her plate down on it as she looked at the food.

There was bread on the plate, that seemed to be the same wherever she went. Next to it was a brown splotch of what appeared to be meat stew. She had no idea what sort of beast it came from but it didn't matter either way. Since there were no eating utensils provided, Melkorka used the bread as a scoop and dunked it into the stew, waiting only a moment for the meaty broth to draw into the bread.

Taking a bite, she finally smiled. The food was good. It was most likely goat and so tender that it dissolved in her mouth. She sucked at the bread as discreetly as possible, trying to retain her dignity even though it had been taken from her on the night of the attack at the fort.

"It's good?" the man asked and Melkorka nodded before she could stop herself.

"I'll have another," he said to the waiting woman who still stood nearby.

Melkorka barely looked up from her meal as the second plate of food arrived. The man sat opposite her, the table between them and she continued to eat in order to avoid having to look at him. However, with the harried action of him scooping up his food and devouring it quicker than she ever could, Melkorka didn't think he was anywhere near interested in her in the present moment.

"My name is Hoskuld," he finally said and Melkorka looked up. He was sucking his fingers, licking the grease from them and Melkorka was repulsed by the action. "And your name is?"

She remained silent, staring at him for a moment longer before ducking her head to her food once more. Hoskuld let her be and she concentrated on eating her food as slowly as possible.

Melkorka was delaying the inevitable. It was likely getting dark outside and, judging by the rowdiness already in the hall, too much ale had been consumed. People would start filtering out, on their way to bed—with or without a companion.

There was no choice in the matter. At some point soon the man would take her away from here to a place where he would bed her and she would have to respond as if she cared for him.

Gilli had made sure to instill that into all of them when they arrived at the market. This was a big gathering, an event that only happened every three years, and men would expect their concubines to be willing. Melkorka had tried not to dwell on what that meant. Locking it away with her voice, she hoped that something would happen, that her father would arrive, or that everyone would suddenly disappear and she would be free.

Obviously, the gods did not listen to her pleas.

"Hey," the man said, his hand reaching out and touching her arm. Melkorka froze against the touch, her food lodging in her throat as the cold dread of her situation stole over her. "I will not hurt you."

Melkorka looked up. She needed to see this man's face as he spoke the words to know if he was lying or not. He was staring at her, his face calm, plain, and not at all deceitful in appearance. Because of this, Melkorka doubted her own reaction even as she felt trust starting to grow.

"I have bought you because I have a wife back home that does not care for me. Sure, we get along just fine but she has no interest in me," Hoskuld started.

Melkorka continued to gaze at him, interested in what he had to say even if his accent was much broader than that she had studied while on the ship. Still, she could understand most of what he said. Hoskuld paused a moment. He picked at something in his teeth before continuing their one-sided conversation.

"I do not want another woman who does not look at me fondly, who does not appear happy when I enter the room. I need someone who will tend to me and who will participate in my life. Do you understand?"

Oh, she understood fully. Melkorka was to be the loving wife he didn't have back home. She was to act and pretend like he was special as if he was better than all of the other brutes in the room. Melkorka could feel her anger rising and she fought against it.

There was only one thing worse than being sold as a slave and that was to be returned. If that were to happen, she would end up on the bottom of the hierarchy and worth nothing more than to shovel excrement and tend to the lowest of tasks. Even in her suffering, she knew that it could definitely get worse—oh, so much worse. So, she fought her ire, shuddering with the task.

In Eriu, they compared a woman's red hair to fire and it wasn't so much as a compliment some of the time. Sure, a redhead could be fiery and passionate, dancing around and warming a man's heart. But she could also be like a wildfire, burning everything in sight.

Melkorka was a wildfire right now. And she had to douse her anger. She had to swallow it down and suppress it or suffer even worse consequences.

She blinked, her gaze still on Hoskuld and she watched as he searched her face. Perhaps, he thought that she was stupid. Or, maybe, he was regretting his purchase. Probably he was thinking both of those things.

Gritting her teeth, she struggled to smile. Her face felt like stone and it was a momentous task to undertake but she somehow managed to spread her lips wide and commit to something that she hoped was endearing.

"Hoskuld!"

Melkorka was started by the word and she looked around, focusing in on a man and a woman. The man was clapping his hand down on her new owner's shoulder. Hoskuld jumped up and allowed the woman to sit before coming around to Melkorka's side and squeezing into the seat there.

The heat of Hoskuld was instant against her side. She still wore the robes that she had worn on the day that she was abducted. Gilli refused to replace her clothes unless she started speaking, for he didn't believe her silent act. However, Melkorka refused. Once again, a way to control the situation. Now, however, after the long sea voyage and having nothing else to wear, her clothing was ragged and dirty. Even as she fought to suppress her anger, she was also thankful for his body heat as it pressed against her.

"Who is this beauty?" the new man asked and slapped his hand down on the shelf between them. It caused Melkorka to jump.

"Careful," Hoskuld replied. "You frightened her."

The man snorted. "Who is afraid of a little slap?"

He raised his hand again and Melkorka watched as he paused above the table and then brought it down swiftly, making a much louder noise than before. She bit at the inside of her lip and tried to brace herself against the noise, her anger flaring once more. The man laughed at her response as did the woman next to him.

"Leave the poor mouse alone," the woman said, more compassionate to her circumstance.

"Seriously, though, where did you find her? She looks like she walked in off the street."

"I purchased her," Hoskuld said quietly, taking a sip of ale as he did so. It was almost as if he were embarrassed to admit it and Melkorka felt shame rising red in her cheeks.

"I hope someone paid you to take her off their hands," the man laughed. "And then gave you more for the lack of decent clothing."

The man pulled at the edge of her robe and strands of cloth came away in his hand. Melkorka darted her hand away from him, hiding it in her lap and couldn't even bring herself to scowl at him. She knew that she looked a mess and suddenly she couldn't work out why she had remained silent all of this time. Gilli would have rewarded her with beautiful new clothing and she would not be sitting here now, humiliated by a brute.

"Enough," Hoskuld said and he beat his own hand down on the bench.

Melkorka jumped once more and closed her eyes, fighting back tears. As she had on countless moments, she wished that she had made different choices. In the present moment, she would give her armband to be anywhere but here. She held her breath, not allowing the sob to be released.

"Hey, it's alright," Hoskuld said in a quiet voice and ran his hand through her hair, smoothing it back in just the way her mother had done when she was little.

She couldn't help herself after that and she fought hard to raise herself up. Pushing past Hoskuld, she felt the heat of him behind her as she brushed him aside.

"For the love of Odin, Veleiv, why do you always have to take it too far?" Hoskuld said.

Once free of him, she battled through the crowd. All the while tears streamed down her face. Bodies were everywhere, jostling against her and making it hard to clear the room. She elbowed a man and another shouted at her as she stepped on his foot. Forcing her way through, could hear Hoskuld calling to her. Melkorka didn't stop. She needed a moment. Or, she needed to escape. Either alternative would work just fine for her presently.

"Hey love," a man leered at her as she worked her way through the thicket of bodies.

Ignoring him, she pushed through the doorway and a rush of cool night air greeted her. Melkorka stopped just as quickly as she had started. Closing her eyes, she could almost imagine that she was home. Sighing, her tears still flowing, she allowed herself this moment to pause, to breathe, to allow the night air to blanket her, and to shock her into this existence.

"I'm sorry about Veleiv," Hoskuld said before she even realised that he had caught up with her. "He can be insensitive."

Melkorka's eyes were still closed but she allowed herself a small nod in acknowledgment. She wrapped her arms around herself and swallowed back a hiccup as her tears slowed.

"There's no need to be so upset," he said.

Reaching up, he wiped away the wetness. His hand stayed there, his warmth bleeding into her own flesh and she leaned into the touch, thankful for the extra heat against the cold night.

"Tomorrow we will buy you new clothes, make you up like the princess that Gilli says you are. And, even if you aren't, you deserve something special. I imagine that you have travelled quite a distance and have seen things you weren't even expecting to see."

Melkorka stared up at Hoskuld. She had come a long way

and seen horrible things. Yet, he had no idea that she was more fearful of what was to come and not what she already knew. But, how could she tell him that? How could he understand that her whole world had been ripped away, her existence replaced and all she had left that remained of herself was the clothes on her back and the armband given to her as a child.

How could he understand that she just needed a moment to work out who she was now?

"Come, let's go to my tent."

Here it was, Melkorka realised as she opened her eyes and looked at Hoskuld. This was when she would have to bed this man and pretend that she liked it. She could feel her heart hammering in her chest and wondered if her new owner could sense her fear.

"Don't worry," Hoskuld said, his hand dropping to her chin as he smiled at her. "I may have paid for a concubine but I am not about to force myself on you. Relax. Tonight, you can sleep in my bed but I do not expect anything from you."

Melkorka was confused by his words and she frowned, which made him chuckle at her. Why would he buy her if he wasn't going to use her?

Hoskuld let go of her chin and took her hand. He led her away from the main hall and down a street between the tents.

"I am set up near the river. It is quieter on the outskirts of the camp and it is better to have fresh water to wash in. Tell me about your homeland?" he said, changing the topic.

He paused for a moment, glancing back at her. His look was quizzical as if he expected her to answer. She tried to speak. The words were there at the back of her throat but it had been such an age that they were locked away and she couldn't cough them up, no matter how much she tried.

Ducking her head, she turned her attention to their interlocked hands. Hoskuld kept a decent grip on her but it didn't seem possessive. Instead, it was merely a guiding support and she wanted to wrap her other hand around his in gratitude for his words.

Hoskuld was nothing like she expected his kind to be and she frowned at the prospect that he might actually be a decent person compared to the stories she had been told and to the events that she had witnessed. He may have bought her but he wasn't amongst the raiders who took her initially. He did not grab at her and slap her around, laughing at their squealing merchandise.

"I suppose you don't want to think about what you have left behind," Hoskuld continued as they walked. "I hope you like my country. Iceland is very different to anywhere you have ever been before."

Melkorka was confused. Was this not his homeland, then? She swallowed back further tears. She couldn't bear the thought of more travelling, of going to a new country, one that was potentially even further away from Eriu.

Hoskuld's words became babble as she tried hard to stop the tears from spilling again. Melkorka felt absurd for her deep emotion in the moment. Still, she didn't know how she was supposed to behave when sold to a man who was not intent on violating her but managed to say every wrong thing regardless.

"We're here," Hoskuld said.

She swallowed once more, the lump in her throat enormous and she wanted to cry against the agony of it. Instead, Melkorka took a deep breath and looked up at her new life.

"It's nothing special, only a travelling hut. But I have some wealth, more than it looks like."

Melkorka stepped into the tent. It was hard to see anything against the dark but her eyes adjusted as Hoskuld stirred up the fire and added more wood. She went to the flames and kneeled, reaching out and warming her hands.

Hoskuld sat across from her and she could feel his eyes burning her just as the flames did when she leaned in closer.

Looking through the flickering light, she saw him, his blue eyes searching, exposing her, and she shivered against it. Melkorka felt uncomfortable with his gaze on her but not because of the primal desire she could identify there but because it reached down inside of her and awoke something that she hadn't felt since the Beltane fire.

Surely, she shouldn't feel this way about him?

Even through all of her fears regarding the Finngaill, she had also heard whispered stories. Melkorka remembered her cousin telling a tale about the beauty of the wild Finngaills and of how they were strong and handsome as well as ferocious and unpredictable. The other girls present had giggled at her cousin's story and swooned about like it would be the most romantic thing in the world to be captured by one of these wild men.

Now, she knew better.

She stared at him, unable to look away, not wanting to even if she could.

The flames flickered between them and Melkorka lowered her hands. Tucking them underneath herself, she sighed as he finally looked away.

"What is your name?" he asked. "At least give me that."

Melkorka wanted to appease him. She wanted to speak and to tell him her name, where she was from, what her life had been like. Yet, she remained silent. Her fear was greater, her need to control something—anything—even greater still.

"Maybe tomorrow, then."

He leaned forward onto his hands. Pushing himself upwards, he stood. Striding across the cramped room, he pulled some extra furs from a box and laid them down on his bed.

"I would offer to sleep on the floor but, as you can see, there is not much room to be had in here. There are plenty of coverings and I will make sure to keep my distance."

He nodded at her and took to his own side of the bed. Pulling off his shirt, he climbed under the covers before

Melkorka really had a chance to acknowledge his chiselled muscles or the way in which the firelight danced across his shoulders.

Turning back to the fire, Melkorka tried to fight the conflicted emotions swirling inside and concentrated on the crackling flames instead.

CHAPTER 6: HOSKULD

HOSKULD TRIED TO SLEEP. HOWEVER, THE warmth of the body next to him—even though they were separated by many furs—distracted him. Already he was regretting his rash decision to buy the woman. And, yet, also he was not. She was silent, mysterious, more beautiful than any woman he had ever laid his sights on.

Still, the way she avoided him, the way in which she had just crept into bed, obviously waiting until he sounded like he was asleep, reminded him so much of his wife, Jorunn, that he clutched at the furs and ground his teeth.

Had he just bought another wife like the one he already had?

Jorunn had been a selection that made sense at the time. It aligned their families and brought together a piece of land that would tie the area closer together, blocking off public access between the community. Not that it stopped people from travelling through but it solidified the location and made those causing trouble to think twice before they crossed the boundaries.

While he and Jorunn had both been in agreeance, they

hadn't known each other very well. It had been fine at the start. Both of them used sex to bridge their differences. However, when the children came along, it had given them the opportunity to grow apart. As life consumed them, they grew apart and when the sex was gone, so too was their common ground.

Jorunn turned to their offspring. Thankfully they had been bountiful in that area and their children prospered under her love and attention. Hoskuld could never fault his wife in that regard.

As for himself? He travelled as often as he could. Even this journey had been designed merely so that he could get away. Although, a little part of his reasoning had been to impress his wife. Even after all these years, he felt the need to try and fix things.

Not that bringing home a concubine would do that. Nor would it mend their disagreement.

Instead, when he finally arrived home with the haul of wood required to tend to their house and to expand it and make it grander than it was now, Jorunn would likely take one look at his new slave and shun them both.

Yes, he had made a mistake.

Still, he listened to the woman's soft breathing. At times it hitched as if she was trying not to cry and he wanted to reach out and take her hand, to tell her that everything was going to be alright. As he was making the same mistakes that he had made with Jorunn, he would do everything within his power to make things better for this woman. She was new linen, perfectly woven and not yet marred with anything. With Jorunn, their cloth was now dirty, patched and stitched over and looking more like this woman's rags rather than something of which to be proud.

The woman sighed and turned over. Her breathing was shallow now as if she were sleeping. Hoskuld turned as well. Her beautiful face was facing him, her brow finally smoothed out, indicating that she really was asleep. A strand of hair had fallen over her face and now lifted and dropped as she breathed. Reaching out, Hoskuld carefully moved it out of the way, her face now fully exposed.

She was exquisite. There was no doubt about that. Jorunn would not only be mad at him but jealous too. In fact, that was likely to be the bigger issue. A concubine was an acceptable prize to bring home after travelling. So, she shouldn't really be upset. Surely, she should understand that it would mean that she didn't have to pretend to welcome him when he approached her on those now rare moments at nighttime. It would give her the very excuse she needed to fully ignore him.

Except that this woman was a glorious creature and Jorunn, who had always been stuck up on how people looked, would likely consider her like a slap in the face. There was no way of hiding the fact that this woman was infinitely more attractive than Jorunn. And, his wife was highly desirable to begin with.

Hoskuld sighed deeply and the woman frowned in her sleep as he did so. He hadn't planned to create such a mess. Yet, he also knew that he might even be overthinking it all.

Perhaps he should just concentrate on making this woman happy before he had to deal with his wife. After all, that was still a long way off. He hadn't even approached the king and requested to harvest wood from the region. It would be a long time before he was ready to return home to Iceland and face Jorunn. This meeting was held so late in the season that he might not even be able to harvest wood before winter set in. If that was the case, he would be here in Denmark over winter before he could travel again. It was plenty long enough to win this woman over and to stop worrying about what his wife would think. With any luck, Jorunn will have found someone else in that time and he would return to find he was divorced anyway.

He could only hope.

And, with that thought, he finally drifted off to sleep.

"HOW ABOUT THIS ONE?" Hoskuld asked as he presented the woman with a dress.

It was the finest that he could find in the marketplace. The robe was made from Russian linen and stitched in a pattern that even he hadn't seen before.

He watched as the woman's eyes lit up.

"We will take it," Hoskuld said to the merchant before he looked for another.

She only had the robe on her back and that one was falling apart. He had wanted her to wash this morning but he figured there was no point in that as she would be dirty as soon as she donned the robe. Instead, they had eaten quickly and headed to the market.

"I need a travelling cloak as well," Hoskuld continued and the merchant scurried off to pull out more items of clothing. "Is there anything you see that you like?"

The woman looked at him and he couldn't work out what she was thinking. "I do not expect anything from you, regardless of how many items I purchase for you today."

He hoped that she would start to trust him. Their beginnings may have been based on a transaction of silver but he didn't want her to think that it meant she was obligated to him.

And, for the life of him, he couldn't work out why it was so important for him that she made the first move towards him. Perhaps he should have bought one of the cheaper women at Gilli's stall. One of those would have surely have approached him by now and be willing to spread their legs for him. They would fake it in just the ways he liked it even though he hadn't told them how to do so.

Yet, deep down, he knew better than that. It would be a hollow connection. In all his life, he hadn't actually had the chance to woo a woman, to treat her as though she were a precious gem or something that needed protecting against the cruel world. Sure, he had tried with Jorunn but she was always so self-reliant that she had fought against those sorts of advancements.

No, he wanted first love and everything that he had seen others in lesser positions go through in order to find a suitable partner for life.

Of course, he understood the reasoning behind why he bought this woman and this woman alone. He knew that she would be a challenge as soon as he set eyes on her impossible beauty. Hoskuld wanted a prize at the end and that was worth so much more in the long run.

The woman had turned away while he got lost in his musings. Now, she fingered other dresses and Hoskuld watched intently to try and work out which dress truly did take her fancy.

She observed all of the robes, spending little time with each of them. That was until she came to a green-hued dress.

She paused for just a moment longer. Her fingers pressing into the material briefly as she closed her eyes before moving onto the next item.

The merchant returned with a dark-coloured cloak and Hoskuld checked to make sure that it was free of faults and thick enough for travel even in the deepest of winters. Not that he thought they would be travelling then but it was better to be prepared for such events than not. To be unready could mean death to those that were not warm enough.

"What do you think of this cloak?" he asked and the woman turned.

She observed it as she closed the gap between them. The scent of her was strong as she approached but his nose did not crinkle against it. He could smell the dirt and dried sweat. However, underneath that was the female aroma of her and it aroused him more than he wanted in such a small confine.

He pushed the cloak towards her, covering his desire as he did so. The woman touched this item as she had done with the others before giving a curt nod.

"Add this to the tally. Plus, that dress there."

Hoskuld pointed to the green one and the woman let out a little strangled noise. He hoped it was a happy sound. Even if she never wore it, he was taking it. This dress meant something to her. Perhaps it reminded her of home and, if it did, he wished that it would bring her some sort of comfort.

The merchant took the item and Hoskuld noticed that the dress featured a stitched pattern reminiscent of that that appeared on the woman's old dress and he decided that it was probably a new dress from her homeland.

So, she really did come from Eriu, then.

Hoskuld hoped to find out more about her soon. He had

no qualms in believing that she might talk to him one day. Sure, she might actually be mute but she seemed to acknowledge his words and understand what he instructed. She just appeared to be traumatised rather than stupid or unable to react. Perhaps the anguish of everything was what caused her not to speak. Or maybe she was merely shy and would open up to him eventually. There was plenty of time to help her to relax and to settle into her new life. And, to trust him. That was the most important thing. He needed her to trust him.

For, without that, she could never grow to love him.

CHAPTER 7: MELKORKA

THE WATER WAS WARM AS SHE LOWERED herself into it. Melkorka had been embarrassed in the beginning as Hoskuld had insisted on helping her. She didn't want to undress in front of him but, as soon as he understood this, he called for another slave woman to help. A thrall, he had called her and she realised that that was her new title now. From the highs of being a princess, she was now the lowest rank of females in this new world of hers.

Even through her despair, the warm water relaxed her and she let out a small moan as she sunk below the surface. She missed this one single little luxury. It would probably now be a part of her job to fill bathing tubs for Hoskuld and the members of his household. Melkorka watched the girl as she poured another jug of hot water into the wooden tub before trudging back to the river's edge and collecting more water.

She wanted to tell the girl that the depth was enough, even though it really wasn't. Her shoulders had gooseflesh raised thanks to the midmorning temperature. Already, she didn't want to trouble people because of her needs, even if others would not do the same to her once she was in Iceland.

Melkorka knew that Hoskuld was married, that his wife was distant. However, she wondered about the other aspects of his life. How many people lived with him and did he have children? Was he in a thriving village or was he a farmer on the outskirts and a vast distance away from the excitement of town life?

The girl returned and poured more water into the cauldron. She supposed it didn't matter regardless and she closed her eyes, letting her muscles loosen in the heat of the water. Melkorka would like to be close to a village with plenty of people around her. Only because it would give her an opportunity to slip away temporarily to gather her own thoughts or, more permanently, if the situation should arise.

She didn't know the penalties for escaped slaves—no, thralls, she was a thrall now—but she imagined that it was severe. So, she had to escape properly or not at all. She also had to remember all of the words, learn as much as she could as knowledge was always power. Or, so her father had told her.

"How is the water?" Hoskuld asked and Melkorka jumped. She opened her eyes and covered her body even though the sides of the tub were high enough to do the job for her—so long as Hoskuld didn't get any closer.

He stayed still, as though he was afraid of startling her. Of course, he wasn't wrong in the matter.

"I have frightened you, I am sorry," he said and backed away until he was closer to their tent than her tub. "Would you like me to leave? I will wait in the tent for you."

She nodded her head and Hoskuld didn't even complain. Instead, he turned and walked away.

A mess of confusion arose. Melkorka felt resentment towards this man, towards her captivity. Yet, somehow, she managed to control him. Was it because she did not speak? Was he truly trying to get her to like him?

Either way, it made a swell of pride rise up. Somehow, in the midst of her anguish, in the prospect of becoming nothing more than a warm body of an evening, she had managed to take control. Because of this, Hoskuld bowed to her and let her have much more freedom than she had ever anticipated.

As he retreated around the side of the tent and disappeared, she regretted telling him to go. If she were to be entirely honest with herself, she could feel an attraction to this man.

Sure, it had everything to do with the way he was built and how his strong arms and broad shoulders were defined without a mark of fat. While his height intimidated her, his broadness did not. And yet, she knew that she should fear his strength more than anything else. Melkorka thought back to the night when the raider had thrown her over his shoulders as easily as if she were a handful of leaves at harvest time.

Then there was his long blonde hair and those impossibly blue eyes that delved into her dreams. Already, she had awoken to them, gazing upon her.

She squirmed in the water as she thought about how she had woken up this morning, her first morning belonging entirely to another person. He had instantly moved back from her face, their distance having only been the length of her hand apart, and gotten out of bed. Before she fully remembered where she was, she knew that she was saddened by the action.

She was attracted to him. And, more likely, the feeling was mutual. That notion left torn in different directions.

Should she escape, Melkorka would leave this man behind.

She would try everything within her means to return to Eriu. There, she would be married to an acceptable man, one of high standing, one that was worthy of her. But, would that man be like this one?

While Hoskuld had paid three times the normal amount for a thrall, it didn't necessarily prove his wealth. And, she knew too well that wealth did not always mean respectability. Gilli had silver aplenty. Yet, she would never consider him for a suitable husband.

Melkorka shook her head. Here she was weighing up her marriage prospects, deciding if wealth and power could match the delicious way in which Hoskuld stared at her. Regardless of who she had been, she had no choice now. She would never marry. Instead, she would merely be the concubine to a man who had bought her with a weight of silver.

The thrall returned and poured more water into the tub but Melkorka was done. She felt jangled, as though she had been thoroughly shaken and wanted to be on the move. Whether it was to visit the market with Hoskuld again or, to find some way to be alone, she didn't care. Although, to be able to run through the woods would be better. She needed to feel physical exhaustion in order to rid herself of all these conflicting feelings. But that would never happen.

No, she would get dressed and return to the tent and do whatever it was that Hoskuld suggested.

ᛘ

"I HAVE TO MEET with King Haakon," Hoskuld said as soon as she entered their quarters.

She was wearing the first dress that Hoskuld had picked

for her this morning. Melkorka couldn't bring herself to wear the green one, the one that had been made in her home country. She wondered if the dress had been a spoil of raids just like she was. Not likely, traders did good business with Eriu. Even she had seen merchants coming to their market to purchase cloth and trinkets to sell in faraway places. No, she was the only spoil of war here.

"Would you like to come with me?" Hoskuld continued and she looked up at him. Before she could even think about it, she nodded her reply. Her master smiled back and grabbed her hand. "Let's go, then."

Melkorka couldn't have pulled away from Hoskuld's grasp even if she wanted to. He was not possessive about his claim with his touch but he held tight regardless and his enthusiasm shone through as he practically dragged her along. She couldn't help but get caught up in his excitement.

"It has been a long time since I have met with the king, and have not yet done so on this visit," Hoskuld explained as they made their way through the centre of the gathering. "He is the reason I am here, though. In fact, that's why we are all here. I guess you don't know much about our way of life, do you?"

Melkorka shook her head as Hoskuld turned back to look at her. He slowed down to match her pace rather than rush ahead.

"We have a gathering every three years so that the king can meet with all of us and so that we can approach him for things that we require. If our standing is important or if the king is generous, he will grant our requests—within reason, of course."

Hoskuld chuckled at her before continuing. "I am after quality wood in order to extend my farmstead. Hopefully, he will grant me this wish. In Iceland, we do not have a lot of decent wood, so have to travel abroad to get it. King Haakon probably has several people requesting the same thing. Not that I am aware of others from my home that have travelled for the same reason but there is always the possibility. Did you know everyone in your country?"

Melkorka scoffed at the question.

There was an impossible number of people that lived in Eriu. She would not know half of them should she meet them. And that was being generous. It surprised her that Hoskuld seemed to know everyone in Iceland. Surely, he was exaggerating? Or, was Iceland really that small that not many people lived there?

Melkorka knew very little about this country. Mostly, the Finngaill were all lumped together and she had never considered them as separate races. All she really thought about regarding them was whether or not they had been sighted raiding close by recently.

"Don't worry, Iceland has plenty of people. We just make sure we know of everyone, well, the important families, anyway," Hoskuld said.

He reached out and ruffled her mess of hair. Melkorka quickly smoothed it all down and tucked what she could behind her ears.

"Your hair is beautiful. You can ask your handmaiden to attend to it if you like. Treat her as you would your own back home. I may have purchased you but you sit well above them as far as thralls go."

Melkorka blushed at his compliment about her hair but was surprised that she held much stead regarding being able to order others around. She didn't know how to respond so she looked ahead at her surrounds. A massive building loomed in front of them.

Hoskuld pointed at the structure. "That's where we're going."

Melkorka nodded and waited as Hoskuld spoke to the guards before pushing through the entrance. Inside, the room was dark compared to outside, even though two fires burned in the centre of the room.

People were gathered around them, some warming their hands, others chatting amongst themselves. It made Melkorka feel hollow, saddened by the fact that she knew no one here.

"That's the king," Hoskuld said.

Melkorka regarded the man seated across the room. He looked just like every other man of importance. He was soft around the edges, obviously used to being protected by his army, and his nose was ruddy as he drank heartily. These sorts of men always seemed to be more carefree than anyone else could be and Melkorka was envious of that.

"There you are, Hoskuld," Veleiv said from beside the king and Melkorka recognised him from the night before.

She ducked behind Hoskuld, her body pressing into the length of the Finngaill. Melkorka was embarrassed by the contact as well as her fear but she was frozen now as if pulling away from him would weaken her somehow. Hoskuld responded by throwing his arm around her.

"Don't mind Veleiv, he will not harm you. I will never allow it."

His voice whispered through her hair, close to her ear, making her shiver with the tickle of his breath as she turned to look at him. He had had to stoop in order to close the distance between them so his face was right in front of her and she could see every line, every scar, every whisker in his long beard.

Hoskuld stared back at her, as though captivated by what he saw and Melkorka turned away. His arm was still around her, though, so she had no choice but to remain by his side. She allowed the heat of him to bleed through, to permeate her clothing as the musky aroma of him made her head swim.

"I have been eager to meet up with you again, Hoskuld," King Haakon said and Melkorka risked another look in his direction. The man's hair was grizzled with grey but was controlled well with a series of braids and beading. "I expected you here much earlier."

The king looked down at them, his gaze darted briefly towards her, obviously disregarding her as a mere woman before he turned back to Hoskuld. Melkorka watched as Hoskuld straightened and addressed the king.

"I am sorry I did not pay my respects immediately, King Haakon," he said. Hoskuld's hand was sweaty in hers but he did not appear outwardly nervous. "There have been family members to visit, ones that I have not seen for many years. You know how we are when it comes to family ties."

The king nodded before beckoning a server over. "Sit with me awhile, eat, tell me what it is that you need."

Hoskuld stepped forward, his arm still around Melkorka and she followed easily as they reached the platform. Veleiv moved over to make room but Hoskuld purposely moved to the other side of the king. "No need to move, Veleiv, there is plenty of space on this side."

There wasn't but Melkorka was thankful that they managed to squeeze in as others shuffled over. She found herself wedged next to an old man who belched at her as she turned to smile at him. However, it was infinitely better than having to be under the scrutiny of Veleiv.

Hoskuld turned to her, further blocking her view of the

man. "You must be hungry, here, help yourself."

He thrust a plate of food at her and she picked at the meat while Hoskuld discussed his request with the king.

Melkorka was glad to be left alone but it gave her more time to think about the way in which she could feel the rock-hard muscles in Hoskuld's thigh pressing against her. It was like sitting up against a boulder, except much warmer. She set her plate down and rested her hand on his thigh since there was no other place for her to place it.

Without looking at her or missing a beat in his conversation with the king, Hoskuld reached over and took her hand. Lifting it to his lips, he kissed it before placing her hand back on his leg, his fingers still laced through hers and her chest swelled in excitement at the action.

CHAPTER 8: HOSKULD

"I WILL GIVE YOU YOUR CLAIM OF TIMBER," King Haakon said and Hoskuld sighed in relief.

Trying to hide it, he took a swig of mead and looked towards his new concubine. The woman was watching the crowd, studying them as if her very life depended on it. And, in a way, it probably did. She needed to learn as much as she could about their culture while she was here so that, when they returned home, there would be no reason for Jorunn to chide her. Turning back to the king, Hoskuld brushed aside thoughts of what would happen when he arrived home with his new woman.

"I thank you, King Haakon. I will be glad to hurry home with the supplies. My wife will be glad when she finds out that she will no longer have to dwell in cramped and leaking conditions."

"This is not your wife, then?" the king asked. "I thought you had finally decided to bring her with you on your travels."

"No, I acquired her recently."

"She is a beauty. What is your name?"

"She does not speak," Hoskuld replied quickly. "She is mute."

The king laughed. "Well, I see you have the best of both worlds, then." Haakon took a long drink before gazing out across the room and the king continued to speak. "I would like you to stay awhile with me. It has been some time since you have shown me service and I always require good men by my side, especially as I fear that this should be our last time together."

"Are you expecting trouble?" Hoskuld asked, surprised. "Since I do not think that you have to worry about age just yet."

The king laughed. "There is always trouble on the horizon with our kind. And, you are too kind regarding my age. We both know that with each passing year, I should be wise to count my blessings. So, I would advise you to seriously consider my offer."

Hoskuld was not surprised at the proposition. It was a great honour to be offered a position in the king's army. With the offer of timber, came a counteroffer and he had known that something of the manner would likely happen.

He seriously considered the king's request. After all, it would mean he would not have to face his wife just yet regarding the new woman. Jorunn would not be happy at the long delay and the thought almost made Hoskuld reply immediately in the affirmative. To see her torn between the honour of the position and having to endure further time in what she considered to be cramped confines, made Hoskuld smile.

"I am sorry," Hoskuld said even though he was regretting the words as they tumbled from his mouth. "But I have obligations at home presently, with my wife and children. I must see to them first before I return to the position. I will be better equipped to take your offer once my farmstead has been expanded."

He was taking a risk and the king could just as likely force Hoskuld's hand by refusing the timber. Although, to have the king insist he stay behind would be better once his wife heard. The difference was in who made the decision.

The king stared at him and Hoskuld wanted to drop his gaze for fear that the king would see the shadows on his words. He could afford to be away from Jorunn for an extended period of time, especially now that he had a new woman to attend to but, if he was being entirely honest with himself, he could not bear to be away from Iceland for that long. Already, he ached for his homeland.

"I understand family obligations," the king replied. "Oh, how I understand them. However, I feel like you perhaps have another reason for rejecting my offer."

"I would love to take you up on your offer, I really would. However, my wife…"

"Wives," he said, shaking his head. "As soon as we are old enough, we are desperate to join with them. However, as we get older, the fun wears off, doesn't it?"

Hoskuld nodded. The king wasn't wrong with his assumption, particularly when it came to Jorunn.

"Although, at the present time, my daughter Briet, seems to cause me more grief than my wife," the king continued. "Your children are young yet. Wait until you have a marriageable daughter who seems to think that adventure is more important than a fine husband."

Haakon laughed and Hoskuld chuckled along with him hoping that the man did not honestly speak the truth. He tried to imagine his daughters causing him trouble but his mind drew a blank.

Slapping his hand down on Hoskuld's leg, the king stood.

"My offer stands once your task is complete. I expect to see you return then."

With that, the king wandered off into the crowd.

Perhaps, he should have taken the position and to Hel with his wife. This new woman by his side could warm his bed eventually, of that he was convinced. Still, it gave him an escape route now if things didn't go smoothly when he returned home.

While she remained silent and still appeared fearful of him, Hoskuld was quietly optimistic. He had noted the swell of her breath beside him after he had kissed her hand. He had seen other glances, too. She may not want to talk and she may also try to appear like she was not fond of him but Hoskuld suspected otherwise.

As he sat, observing the crowd and left to his own thoughts, Hoskuld strummed his thumb over the woman's hand. He revelled in the softness of her skin under his touch.

He wanted to lay with her, his body craving it. However, he was not going to push the matter. Hoskuld wanted her to want him, not be forced into the situation.

Turning, Hoskuld saw the dart of her eyes as she kept her head forward but also kept him within her sight. Already, she knew exactly where he was and what he was doing. She would make a good thrall. But he wanted so much more than that. He required someone who would be interested in him and who would share his life.

"Now that the king has granted permission to mill wood, we will be heading off as soon as the gathering breaks up on the morrow," Hoskuld said, wanting to kiss her hand once more but refraining. He didn't want to seem too eager and frighten her off.

Turning towards him, her gaze settled squarely on his face. She looked at him honestly and without fear. It was an improvement and he hoped it was her new normal and not just an accident.

"I imagine that you are worried about travelling and meeting my family?"

Hoskuld paused, hoping that she would answer but she simply nodded. He reached up and tucked a strand of hair behind her ear, brushing his fingers along her chin before breaking contact.

"I have several young children," he continued. "The youngest was born not long before I set off on this journey. He is the reason Jorunn wants more room. Although, I can't see why. Our home is large enough as it is. There is plenty of space for all of us as well as for other guests. However, what my wife wants, she gets most of the time."

Hoskuld shrugged. "To be honest, I am not sure just how Jorunn will react to your arrival. I am hoping that she will be fine with it. There is nothing wrong with bringing home a new thrall, after all. Not for our kind. I hear it is different elsewhere. How is it in your country?"

Once again, there was no answer.

"Please don't think that you will be shamed for being sold to me. We do not have the same ideas of the Christians yet and do not care so much for keeping relations entirely within the marital bed. Although, their religion is sneaking in. I have seen it on my travels and I have even seen it here at this gathering."

It made Hoskuld sad to think that the old ways could be overtaken by the new god of the Christian faith. Those following Christ seemed so scared all the time. Scared to die, scared to live, scared that they were not good enough in the eyes of their All-Father. His faith was much easier, more honest, and he did not want it to change.

"Thralls can have quite a good life, even under the rule of another. Some even become free citizens. And, that is how I would like you to think of the situation. You may not be entirely free but I expect you to have your own thoughts and feelings. I want you to explore my world and to settle into it. Always remember that if my wife choses to object it is because she can and not because there is anything wrong with bringing home someone such as yourself."

Hoskuld continued to rub his thumb over the soft skin of her hand. Her fingers twitched, as though she were squeezing his hand, as though she was doing it on purpose. His chest swelled and he hoped that something could grow of this. As he gazed upon her face and observed her watching the action of his hand against hers, Hoskuld promised to himself that if he could not successfully woo this woman, he would set her free.

She was so fine, so exquisitely beautiful that she didn't deserve to be owned. He wanted to set her free now but was scared that someone else would latch onto her and take possession. No, he would protect her for as long as he could and, if after all that time, she decided that she did not desire him then he would let her go. They had plenty of land and she could settle independently of them and have her own life. Regardless, Hoskuld would look over her and protect her even if she was no longer his to own.

✗

IT WAS DARK AS they left the great hall. Hoskuld had feasted and met with many people that he had not seen for a very long time. His new woman had sat patiently by his side even though he gave her leave to wander if she so desired.

Now, he was drunk and staggered slightly, his arm around her as he tripped through the marketplace. Tonight, the streets were as busy as if were daytime. It was always this way on the last day of the gathering.

"We will be up at first light," Hoskuld said as he gazed up at the moon. It was almost full, the perfect time to travel. Not that they would be going far before stopping once more but it was always easier when the night was lit up by the moon.

Hoskuld let go of the woman and teetered off to one side to relieve himself. He spoke to distract himself.

"It will only take a day or so to reach Booths'-Dale, which hosts the type of timber that I require. We will then settle down until enough wood has been felled."

Hoskuld was babbling, he knew that. Yet, this woman did that to him. He wanted to tell her everything, even the mundane things, especially those. They had so much to learn about each other and he wanted to share it all at once.

He stopped talking as he finished up, turning, he came face to face with the woman. Standing still, she was gazing up at the sky. She looked mesmerized and Hoskuld came to stand next to her.

"You like the moon," he said quietly before taking her hand once more. "I like it also. We call him Mani. His brother is Sol, the sun."

She turned to look at him, so he continued on. "Every day, Sol's horses are chased by a warg called Skoll. During the night, his sister, Hati, does the same to Mani. During Ragnarok, it is said that they will finally meet. Because of this, Sol and Mani will be no more and we will all be plunged into darkness as the gods battle each other."

She gasped at his words and Hoskuld focused in on her once more. "It is a brutal story, for a brutal breed of people, I imagine you are thinking right now."

She nodded at him and Hoskuld was glad for her honesty. He reached over and took her chin between his thumb and forefinger. "I always want you to be truthful with me. I do not care if your thoughts are different to mine or if you object to what I have to say. Honesty from you is more important than your praise."

Leaning in, he risked a kiss. Keeping his eyes open, he centred his gaze on hers, watching as the realisation snuck across her face. Still, she continued to look at him as he approached and he was hopeful for her embrace.

Her lips were soft and parted slightly when they met. The sweet softness caused his to close his eyes. He groaned into the touch as her lips crashed against his and he wanted more. His hand was still on her chin and he guided her towards him as he reached up to caress her fiery hair.

Stepping closer, his body melding into hers and the feel of her breasts against his chest was more than enough to make his arousal grow. She closed her eyes and he was happy that she seemed to be enjoying this. Opening his mouth further, he probed at her. Her lips started to soften, to comply before she suddenly pushed him away.

Hoskuld groaned at the disruption, as he came back into the present. He tried to pull her back towards him but she resisted and he let go, his fingers trailing down her arm as he tried for one last moment to feel the glory of her.

"I am sorry," he said, stepping backward, his body fighting against his head with such a ferocity that he nearly succumbed and forced himself upon her. "I-I have had too much to drink and shouldn't have done that. It will not happen again until you want me to."

She nodded at him and for a moment he thought he saw her hesitation, as though she regretted having pulled away when she did. His breath hitched as his raging erection pushed against his trousers.

Still, he would not push the matter. He had to let her be, to allow her time to adjust to him, to her new life.

Her new life.

It suddenly dawned on him just how difficult this all must be for her. "Truly, I am very sorry."

He stepped away from her and walked quickly to their hut, allowing her time to be by herself.

CHAPTER 9: MELKORKA

MELKORKA REMAINED OUTSIDE AND underneath the comfort of the moon well after Hoskuld's departure. She raged with emotion as Arianrhod's orb blanketed her with its soft glow.

Hoskuld had just kissed her.

And, she had kissed him back.

Well, for the briefest of moments until her absurdly rational mind had taken over and insisted that she should not embrace with the very brute that had bought and now owned her. But, for the sweetest of moments, his warm lips against her own had been bliss.

Hoskuld's embrace was so much gentler than she had thought a man like him could be, His brawn, along with his hard and chiseled muscles, had her automatically assuming that he would be hard all over.

And, he was, mostly.

In fact, she had felt how much so he was in a certain spot and it made her stomach flip over with pure excitement. If only she could go back to the moment when he had drunkenly leaned in and her world shrank down to nothing but the sight of his blue eyes.

Looking up at the moon, almost ready to burst with its pregnant size, Melkorka prayed to Arianrhod that her life would work out, that she would know what to do.

Oh, how she wanted to embrace Hoskuld. She wanted to march on over to their hut and plant another kiss on his lips. Yet, she was frozen to the spot as she fought against her inner turmoil.

Melkorka reasoned that she should not be feeling this way about him. All her life she had been told about how terrible his kind was, that they were only after wealth, fame, and the flesh of women.

The rumours seemed to be right about them wanting flesh. But, didn't all men? It was the same at home. Men were interested only in what was between a woman's legs. Most of their time seemed to be spent travelling to that very point— even when planning war, even when in the midst of war.

Perhaps she needed to be more like the men surrounding her, both here and at home. Maybe she should just take control of her life. Hoskuld had told her that was possible, even as his thrall.

She was allowed to have her own opinion and to disrespect him if she felt it warranted. Yet, she didn't know that she believed him fully. It was one thing for a man to say he liked a woman who fought against his opinion, it was another thing entirely when you were telling him that his ideas were terrible or that she didn't want to bed him even though she had in the past.

Melkorka had seen it many times before. Men who thought it was fun to have a fiery woman by their side. Until they were disagreeing with them. Her own father had complained continuously when she had objected to his ideas. Melkorka had been safe in fighting back against him. Yet, here, with a man she had only known for a few days, it was something else entirely. She didn't want to find out the hard way; not in a land where no one knew her or wouldn't notice if she wasn't there anymore.

A cloud came over the moon and Melkorka turned towards the tent. Hoskuld was in there, possibly still awake but, just as likely, passed out after drinking so much. She had

had several drinks herself but had turned the flagon away once she felt the buzz of alcohol come over her. Melkorka didn't want to fall into something she would regret on the morrow.

Or, maybe she did.

She kicked at a stone as she moved off and the clouds cleared, lighting her way once more. Each step took her closer to what might happen, an impossible moment that dragged away into eternity but also, somehow, as quick as a rabbit bounding across the field with a fox hot in its pursuit.

The scratch of the door as she pulled it aside grated across her heart and she felt the presence of what had just happened between them, of Hoskuld, her captor, her Finngaill. Somehow, he felt like her redemption. Melkorka wanted it as much as she didn't and she wondered what she would be doing now if she were home.

It was a simple answer. She would be sleeping, safe in the knowledge that her life was mapped out for her. Ina would continue to dote on her and, eventually, a suitor would come. Her father would agree if the price and prestige was high enough. Then, she would be shipped off to become a wife and a mother.

It was a different kind of captivity. The acceptable kind.

She crossed the room, slipping off her boots once she reached the bed platform. Pulling off her dress, she left her underclothes on.

As she sank into the furs, her mind raced, not sure of what would happen and suddenly not even caring. She would let this night unfold as it would. Her kind believed that your destiny could change. The Finngaills did not. She had discovered this from the travelling bard who told bold stories of those who had tried to change their preordained fate. If their stories were true it meant that she belonged here, that this fate was always hers to own.

"I am still awake," Hoskuld said as Melkorka pulled the furs up to her neck.

He turned towards her, his arm settling over the top of the coverings, an impossible weight. The furs were so thick that he could not possibly feel her skin beneath but Melkorka felt his touch all the same as it burned through the pelts and sizzled into her.

She turned, her body twisting underneath his arm until his fingers rested on her waist. Melkorka wished that her arm was also over the coverings and that Hoskuld would run his fingers over her bare flesh. He liked to touch her, to always have his skin upon her own, even if it was not in a sexual or possessive way.

Already, she missed it.

And, as if he knew her very thoughts, his hand reached up, arcing in the firelight and Melkorka held her breath as she waited for it settle on her cheek. His fingers were soft against even though she could also feel the calluses of hard work and war upon his palm.

"You are beautiful," he said and Melkorka closed her eyes. "Never forget that."

Melkorka was not sure of how to react to the compliment. She knew what normally followed such words and she fought against her normal reaction. Her body helped as it rose up, ready to respond to whatever came next.

"I am sorry about before. I forget that you are not of my kind, that this is all new to you. Please, tell me to stop if I am going too fast, or if you need to find out more about what is going on. I want to show you everything and to help you to fall in love with my world. I suppose that you have been completely overwhelmed with everything."

His fingers traced along her jaw as a shiver of delight coursed through her. Opening her eyes again, she swam in his gaze. His eyes were the only thing in this world, the only thing that mattered, anyway.

He leaned in once more and Melkorka did not flinch, she did not fight against her own thoughts. Instead, she welcomed their kiss. Hoskuld kept his eyes open, just as she did.

Exposed by the moment, she was bare and ready for the taking by this man that she had only just met. Melkorka wanted him to devour her, to take her completely and own her in a multitude of ways. Blushing at her thoughts, she was surprised at just how much passion was now rising to the surface with their kiss.

Reaching up, she bought her hand out from under the blanket and rested it against Hoskuld's. Her fingers traced the veins along the back of his hand as she began the journey of learning his body.

He closed his eyes and Melkorka felt the loss of it. Their embrace deepened, his mouth parting and lips softening as his tongue darted out. She trembled under the flickering touch. As soon as Hoskuld noticed this, his embrace slackened.

Melkorka wanted to scream against it. She wanted him to kiss her deeply, to run his hands along her body, exposing her bare flesh as he did so. Her desire was mounting and she could feel it pulsing between her legs even though they barely touched. Pulling back slightly, their lips were now separate and Melkorka felt wretched tears fighting their way to the surface.

"I do not want to harm you."

Hoskuld's words were hot against her lips and she swallowed hard. His fingers traced along her jaw, leading their way lower as she felt the shiver of it against her neck. Melkorka wanted to reach in, to devour him with her kisses but found that she could not.

She wanted to open her mouth and let the words tumble out. Melkorka wished she could tell him that it was alright, that he could touch her, that he could explore her and she wouldn't mind. However, her tongue had a mind of its own and remained clamped to the roof of her mouth.

Hoskuld pulled back, the distance between them opening up and she felt a rush of cold air like a wall being built between them. "I will not push you any further."

Tears welled in her eyes and she blinked them back, unable to open her eyelids once they were shut for fear that they would spill over and trickle down her face.

Hoskuld must have seen her anguish for his strong arms wrapped around her. Snuggling in, it was the one small concession that her body allowed.

He kissed the top of her head and pulled her around so that her back was pressed against his chest. His fingers laced into hers as his arms held her tight.

Down low, she could feel his arousal and she wanted to squirm against it as the heat left its mark against her hip.

"Sleep, my precious one," Hoskuld whispered into her ear and the hotness of his breath shot straight through her and she feared that she would never be able to sleep again unless he sated her desire for him.

Her tears finally escaped. Melkorka allowed them to fall, soaking into the furs beneath them. Her sobs, however, she choked back until Hoskuld spoke once more.

"Cry," he said. "Let it all out. I will not be offended."

And so, she did.

At first, the sobs were quiet, mewling little sounds that she allowed to drift out slowly and carefully. However, as Hoskuld's arms tightened and his body wrapped further around hers, she felt safe enough to let the howls follow.

Her nails dug into the furs and into Hoskuld's hand when he offered it. She clutched tightly to the man that she had only known for the shortest of times and felt secure. Against all the odds, Hoskuld made her feel sheltered from the world. For the first time, she believed that she could trust him and that he could do the same in return.

Melkorka didn't know for how long she cried. All that she knew was that Hoskuld allowed it. He didn't try to soothe her, or to use hollow words telling her that everything was going to be alright. Neither did he tell her to calm down or to be quiet lest someone should hear her. Instead, he just kissed her hair and allowed her misery to flow.

CHAPTER 10: HOSKULD

THE DAY WAS CLEAR AS THEY SET DOWN AT Booths'-Dale. Hoskuld alighted immediately, skipping across the beach before turning and waiting for his new woman.

A storm had kicked up and the travel had not been kind to her. She had been seasick for a lot of the time. Even Hoskuld had felt a little uneasy at certain points in the journey.

The woman staggered once and Hoskuld rushed up to help her. She leaned on him and he was glad that she was finally trusting enough to do so. It had been a slow process and he thought back fondly on the last night they had spent in Denmark.

He had wanted more but hadn't pushed her. In fact, he suspected she had also wanted the same thing and, since then, he swung between knowing that he had done the right thing and kicking himself for not taking advantage of the situation. If his brother-in-law were to know, Hoskuld knew exactly what he would have said about the situation.

"We only have to travel a little distance before we can stop but, if you are too unwell, we can settle here for a while."

"Gotten her with child already, have you?" Thord asked,

tapping him on the shoulder as he passed. Others around them laughed at the comment and Hoskuld watched as the woman scowled.

"Ignore them," Hoskuld whispered discreetly into her ear.

Leading her to a large boulder, Hoskuld allowed her to sit for a moment and gather herself. He could see her swaying, as though they were still on the water. Sometimes it took a while for the sensation of the waves of the ocean to leave a person once they settled on land again.

As she leaned over, finally ready to vomit once more, Hoskuld grabbed her hair and held it back from her face.

"There you go," he said with a chuckle. "We can head off shortly."

The others on board gathered their equipment while Hoskuld sat with the woman.

"Ready?" he asked after a while.

Nodding at him, she stood. She was a little frail but squared her shoulders as though determined not to be counted as a weak woman.

"We should reach those trees by midday," Hoskuld said as he pointed to a dense copse far ahead.

The woman nodded at him; her face grim with determination.

"You can rest, or explore, or whatever you feel like once we reach it. We will set about immediately to cut down enough trees for my farm. Hopefully, this leg of our journey will only extend a few weeks."

The woman smiled at him and he reached out and took her hand. She trembled slightly in his grasp and he put an arm around her shoulders as they walked. Leaning into him for a while, she eventually pulled back as her strength returned. She did not release her hold on his hand, though, and Hoskuld smiled at the gesture.

"I can't wait for you to finally see Iceland. It is quite different from what you have already seen of Denmark and now here in Norway. We don't have such a covering of trees like here, that's why we need to travel abroad for supplies. However, if you struggled with the distance by boat, you might find the trip across the Norwegian Sea to be even more challenging. Although, if the gods favour us, we should reach Iceland in only a matter of days."

They walked the remainder of the distance in silence after that. The woman seemed more interested in observing the landscape and Hoskuld left her to do so.

When the copse finally loomed in front of them, the atmosphere in the group picked up significantly. Hoskuld let go of the woman's hand and set forth to start marking trees for felling.

"Can you sort out a meal before we start?" Hoskuld asked of the woman and she nodded, immediately pulling dried traveling food from one of the packs

"Do you want me to see if I can hunt up some fresh meat for the evening meal?" Thord asked as they sat around eating. Hoskuld nodded his reply.

After the meal was finished, Thord took Einar with him and set off in pursuit of prey. The other men regarded Hoskuld as his woman cleared things away.

Hoskuld looked at the tall trees. He was excited to finally gather supplies. His farm would prosper thanks to Jorunn's insistence on expansion. He may not have initially wanted to make the trek but he knew that it would be good for them, that it would help to further build their reputation and create a better holding within society.

Looking back, pride swelled. He had a good group of men.

Some he had known since he was a child. Others had married into his family and joined with him as they battled warring factions. Others still, like Birgir, had only recently joined his group. Birgir was one of King Haakon's men, tasked with keeping an eye on them, no doubt, but he appeared reliant. Plus, he was a hard worker and eager to help out now that they had landed.

Hoskuld was lucky. All of these men supported him. Many, like Thord, would remain with him at his farmstead once the building was completed. Others would return to their homes. Birgir, he suspected would stay a while before returning to report back to the king. Hoskuld would make sure that there was nothing ill to say about him.

"What do you plan to do while we work?" Hoskuld asked of the woman. She shrugged her reply. "You can travel afoot if you like. Feel free to explore the location. It is safe here. Take one of the men if you feel like you may need protection. However, very few people travel this way unless it is for timber, so you should be free of other people."

Hoskuld watched the woman as she looked out across the landscape before wandering off towards the trees. He hoped that she would be safe, that there really was no one else out there.

"Here, take this," Hoskuld said and he pulled his knife free from its place at his waist.

The woman looked at the weapon before her gaze travelled upwards to meet his. She nodded and took it, tying the sheath to her waist before she left.

THE FIRE CRACKLED, LIGHTING the darkening sky with its intensity. It had been a long day and the huge bonfire was a way to show their respects to the gods for supplying them with their bounty.

Hoskuld sucked a bone, enjoying the meat. Thord and Einar had managed to bring down a female goat and its suckling kid. They had spilled the blood of the beasts over the wood before lighting it as an offering.

He was exhausted. Having travelled so far for the meeting and then the time spent here, he had grown soft and his muscles ached in response to the hard work.

As he ate, he tried not to make it obvious that he was looking out for the woman. She had been gone all day and it was fast approaching nighttime. Hoskuld hoped that she hadn't come to blows.

A nagging feeling that she had left him far behind and was now a free woman enveloped him. Hoskuld hoped that this was not the case. To do so would make her life much worse than she likely thought it was already. A thrall had many more rights than an escaped thrall. And, if she were to approach a town, they would know that she was not one of them, that she was likely an escapee and the judgment would be harsh.

"Your little woman seems to have deserted you," Birgir said as he slumped down beside him. "Here, you need a drink."

Hoskuld took a swig from the bladder before returning it.

"Leave Hoskuld alone," Thord said. "He already has one terrible wife, do not wish another on him."

Hoskuld nodded and raised the bladder towards his friend. They had grown up together and now lived close by to each other. Together, they shared a past as well as a problem; both suffering from wives that did not seem to care for them.

"Odin knows that no one should be inflicted with wives such as ours, not even our enemies," Hoskuld said.

The ale was loosening his tongue. Normally he would not speak as such towards Jorunn. However, within the company he was keeping, and with no other women about to listen in and gossip, he felt safe to finally reveal details of his marriage. As he did so, the wight of his secret, one that everyone knew but never spoke of, lifted form his shoulders.

"Well, maybe our *worst* enemies," Thord said as he took the drinking vessel and had a swig from it.

Everyone laughed and Hoskuld settled back, smiling as the banter continued until a noise in the brush had distracted him. A second snap of a twig then saw every man reach for his waist, ready to grab their weapons. Hoskuld's knife was absent but he had another dagger at his ankle that would suffice.

The silence now deafening as it swallowed up the merriment.

Another noise and then the woman appeared. Stepping towards the fire, she reached out, her hands stretching towards the warmth. The men surrounding her relaxed and she didn't even seem to notice that they were ready to use their weapons if required.

The woman took the food and sat down next to him. Quickly, she took a bite, chewing rapidly before swallowing.

"How was your day?" Hoskuld, but no answer followed, it never did. Still, he tried to engage her, to catch her by surprise. One day she might accidentally answer him. "I hope you didn't run into any trouble."

Hoskuld searched her body for signs of injury. Her hair had a few leaves caught in its fiery masses but there was no other indication there that she had run into any great strife.

Her clothes were clean, undamaged, and Hoskuld breathed a sigh of relief.

"Did you find your way back here easily?" That was his other fear, that she had become disoriented and lost her way somehow.

The woman nodded her reply and Hoskuld was relieved.

"Then, I wish that you would tell me what you saw. Norway is filled with waterfalls. I wonder if you came across any of them. Some are quite impressive. If we have a free day, I should like to show you some. However, I suspect we will not have the time on this trip. We need to travel before winter gets close. It is too treacherous otherwise. In order to return home before then, we have a very limited time in which we can work here. I will be turning in soon but feel free to stay up as late as you like. We'll all be up early on the morrow so that we can set back to work."

Hoskuld stood and headed towards his traveling tent. It was much smaller than the one he used at the meeting and he had to bend down to pass through the entrance. With his days being spent cutting down trees, there was no need for any of the luxuries that went with his other tent. This one didn't even have room for a fire to be built inside and his breath puffed out with the coldness as he quickly clambered under the furs.

Even as he settled, he heard a disturbance at the doorway and smiled as the woman entered.

"There is not much room in here and it is cold but, trust me, I will not harass you. However, I cannot say that I will not come close while I sleep if I need to keep warm."

He figured honesty was the best thing given the situation.

The woman said nothing as she huddled down low and pulled off her tunic. She grabbed at the covers as soon as she was free of her outerwear and jumped underneath the furs. Hoskuld wriggled over to give her some extra room but she scooted across to him, diving into his chest and wrapping her arms around him for warmth.

Hoskuld kissed the top of her head and returned the favor by enclosing her within his arms. As he drifted off to sleep, he couldn't wipe the smile from his face.

CHAPTER 11: MELKORKA

MELKORKA AWOKE TO FEEL HOSKULD'S ARMS around her. She grinned as she snuggled down further.

Most of the wood had been felled over the past few weeks and Hoskuld had kept to his word that he would not push her to consummate their relationship. Which meant that she wanted it so bad that she could taste it.

She bit down on her lip as she squirmed into the sleeping man, wondering just how far she could push him before he ravished her against her will. Not that it would actually be against her will.

Hoskuld's breathing changed as she pushed back into him and she knew that he was waking. She paused in her task, holding her breath to see what would happen next.

"You will be the death of me, woman," he said and her smile broadened.

Pulling back the furs, he rolled out of bed. "You had better be careful what you are proposing because one day I will take you up on your offer and then I will never be able to resist you again."

Melkorka pulled the furs up over her face, biting into the rough of it and trying not to squeal. By the time she had lowered the pelts, he was gone and the room felt empty without him.

She followed his action and got out of bed, not really knowing what she would do with her day. Melkorka had previously searched the forest, revelling in being alone, thankful that Hoskuld allowed her the freedom.

On the first day, she had walked as far as she could in one direction, just to see if she could find a village. She had no luck and had found herself returning as the sky darkened. It had scared her a little, being out in a foreign land as the sun sank lower in the sky. When she had finally burst into the camp, she had sighed in relief, glad that she had found their camp.

Hoskuld had never scolded her for being out so long, neither had he since. Instead, he allowed her the very freedom that she craved. Ever since that day, the need to escape had dulled. Hoskuld trusted her, even more so than her father ever had. Beyond that first warning and the acknowledgment that she might need a weapon, Hoskuld had never spoken again of the dangers that lurked in the wilds.

And why should he? They were in Norway, homeland of the Finngaills and there was no one wilier than them when it came to raiding. When you took the raiders out of the situation, there was no reason to risk being alone in the countryside.

As she observed the men, as they spoke of their wives and lovers, she realised that that was the way of them. Women were given more freedom than in Eriu. They were trusted and allowed more privilege than her own womenfolk. It made her want Hoskuld more in the knowledge that she was getting a better life as a captive to the Finngaill than she was ever likely to receive at home.

Still, the notion that her abduction was the best thing that could have ever happened to her gave her mixed feelings. She should still resent what had happened, not enjoy the notion that it wasn't just Hoskuld that treated her that way. Beyond the initial ribbing from Hoskuld's men, they had settled down quickly and she was simply accepted into their tribe. Melkorka fetched their food and moved the smaller branches that were scattered around the place due to all the fallen timber. She helped out where she could, and the men respected and thanked her for the help.

She hoped that it would be the same when they finally reached Iceland and Hoskuld's wife met her. Melkorka had noticed the other men occasionally making reference to Jorunn and how she would not be fond of her. This was the single thing that worried her as the days marched quickly towards the journey to Hoskuld's homeland.

Watching Hoskuld, she could see him nodding in agreement with the others regarding his wife. All the time, he smiled at her and told her that everything would be alright because Jorunn had no right to complain about her presence.

Still, she fretted.

What if she and Hoskuld did become lovers and Jorunn wanted to put a stop to that? Melkorka could already feel her attraction growing into something more than just lust. Sure, she wanted to make love to the man, to lay with him and cherish him merely because her body was hungry for his. Yet, there was something else. Hoskuld had treated her nicely, making sure that she fitted in and was treated just as well by the others in the group. To have him reject her in order to return to his wife and turn his back on her would be a devastating blow.

As Melkorka stepped out of the tent and walked across to the fire, she smiled at the men as she passed. Many of them assumed that she had slept with Hoskuld already. They were wrong but she didn't make an objection. Instead, she allowed their banter and innuendo, bobbing her head downward as though embarrassed.

Melkorka was handed a plate of stew that was left over from last night. As she sat, she ate quickly, glad for the warmth of it. The days were still warm when the sun was high but the temperature quickly plummeted as soon as it dipped below the mountain range circling them.

Hoskuld was nowhere to be seen so Melkorka concentrated on her food. She listened to the men, their accents no longer thick and hard to understand. Instead, they sounded normal to her now. They talked about the day ahead, of the work that must be undertaken. The weather and the change of the season were also strong in conversation, as was general praise for Hoskuld.

So far, Melkorka had yet to meet a person who had anything bad to say about the man who owned her. Instead, everyone liked him, even Birgir, who was obviously under instruction from the king. She could understand why, though. After all, a man could always be valued on how he treated his slaves, her father had said and Hoskuld was the perfect example of a man who lived up to this virtue.

Hot breath caressed her ear as her hair was swept aside. Turning, Hoskuld greeted her with a kiss to her cheek. She wished that his lips had managed to brush against her own.

"What are you up to today?" he asked as he sat down next to her. His hand sought out hers and she clapped her own down on top of his, owning him and making sure that he was trapped by her.

She shrugged out her answer, still not willing to speak aloud. Melkorka had reached a point where she wasn't even sure that she could speak anymore. Over the last few days, she had tried when she was out in the wilds and far away from the group. Her voice had rasped and hurt her throat so she gave up after the first attempt. She didn't need her words anymore, anyway, she reasoned at the time.

"Well, have a good day, then," Hoskuld said and stood. Melkorka held tight and he laughed at her. "The sooner I set to work, the quicker it will be done and I can return here. Trust me, I miss you too."

Melkorka continued her hold. Her fingers laced through, squeezing his fingers. He looked down at her, imploring, as she tugged at his arm. She pulled his hand towards her, their gaze never breaking, as she kissed his knuckles.

Hoskuld licked his lips and desire flared, even Melkorka could sense it.

Lowering down onto one knee, Hoskuld came face to face with her. She could see that he wanted her, that his need for her had grown with her single action.

"I will be back as soon as I can," Hoskuld said as he leaned in closer. "And, when I do, I want to ravish you. Take this as your final warning to be free of me."

Melkorka shivered with his words before nodding at him.

Hoskuld moved in further, his hot breath on her face now as his gaze continued to delve into her. "I want you," he said before their lips met.

Melkorka wrapped her arm around his shoulders and pulled him in, surprised with her brazen action.

She was done with waiting. Hoskuld had proved himself to her and she was ready to go further. If she did not do it now, she had no doubt that it would never happen once they reached Iceland and his wife was back in his life.

Hoskuld groaned into their kiss and the noise resonated through her. She could feel it diving deep down into her core and a dampness between her legs made her smile into their embrace. Pulling away, he kissed her once more, quickly, before unravelling his hand from her grasp.

"I must go now," he said. "Until I return."

$$\text{Λ\kern-0.3em\Lambda}$$

WANDERING BETWEEN THE CAMP and the beach, Melkorka had spent a lot of the day gazing out to sea, lost in the hugeness of it. She felt tiny, insignificant by its presence. Yet, at the same time, she could feel its power as it swelled on the beach, lapping at her ankles when she let it.

Melkorka had never been attracted to the ocean before, preferring the green of the forest, the closed-in feeling of protection that the trees gave. Yet, this was her new life now. The Finngaill were travellers, sea voyages were an oft occurrence and something she would likely have to get used to.

Or, perhaps, she would be left behind like Jorunn was now.

She didn't like that idea. Now that she had attached herself to Hoskuld, she didn't want to be left behind. She would not allow it, she decided, as she picked up a pebble and threw it out to sea. The stone skipped across the water before sinking below the surface and she felt just like it. Dancing across the water, hoping not to fall, to not be swallowed up by the dangers in plain sight. Yet, she also knew that Hoskuld was not a danger to worry about. He would keep her afloat.

"I bet I can make my stone go further," Hoskuld said and Melkorka turned. Once again, she was startled by how he could sneak up on her, about how lost inside her own thoughts she could truly be.

Reaching down, Hoskuld selected another pebble before hefting it and skipping it across the water. A wave kicked up unexpectedly and engulfed the stone before it truly had a chance to stretch out across the water.

"Well then, maybe not."

He came to stand beside her, his hand reaching out to grasp hers and Melkorka melted into him. She leaned her head on his chest as she continued to look out over the water.

"Iceland is over there," he said, pointing out across the sea and she followed his direction. "I can't wait for you to see it. It is a magical land, like no other place you will ever see."

Melkorka sighed, scared about the trek for a variety of reasons. She wondered at just how seasick she would be as they crossed the open waters. Also, she was worried about meeting Jorunn and the rest of Hoskuld's family. What would his children think of her? Or his community?

"I spoke the truth this morning when I said that you are no longer safe with me."

Melkorka closed her eyes briefly, her heart hammering in her chest. Lifting her head, her eyes opened so that she could gaze upon him before she reached up to kiss him.

She was ready and she did not want him to question her attraction to him any further. Melkorka needed him and she wanted him to know that.

"Last chance," Hoskuld said through their kiss and Melkorka allowed her tongue to dart out and silence him.

His arms wrapped around her, enclosing her into his embrace and sheltering her from the cold wind coming straight off the sea. Her fingers trailed over his waist, trying to feel his physique through his many layers of clothing.

Hoskuld's hands tangled in her hair, pulling her closer and their kiss deepened. She stared deep into his gaze, his blue eyes competing with the colour of the sky behind him. He pulled away, looking at her like he had never seen her before, as though she was a new acquisition.

And, in a way, she was.

"I need you," he said, his voice as hoarse as hers when she had tried to speak out in the wilds all those days ago.

Melkorka reached up, her fingers trailing over his cheek and he leaned into her touch. Standing tall, she kissed the tip of his nose before searching for his lips once more.

Hoskuld grabbed at her, a groan erupting from deep down inside and it resonated just as deeply inside of her. His arms wrapped around Melkorka, lifting her up, cradling her as they continued to kiss.

She was hungry now. Grabbing at him, her fingers tugged at his braids, pulling him against her. They were clamped together yet she still felt like they were not near enough. Melkorka wanted to be closer. She wanted him inside of her, the closest that anyone could ever be with another person.

Hoskuld's arms were tight around her, his fingers cradling her and she wished to be naked under his touch, for his fingers to be digging into her flesh and not her clothing.

He broke free of their kiss and smiled at her. "I need to

see where I am going. However, once we reach our tent, I will not break hold again."

Melkorka felt her desire swell as tears threatened. She was not sad; her emotions were merely scattered all over the place. Wanting him so badly that her knees trembled, she was glad that he held her, that he was carrying her through the sand and towards their tent.

She was also scared. Not at what was about to occur but because she knew that others would be aware of what was happening and she felt her embarrassment already forming. Still, she allowed Hoskuld to take her. Hiding her head in his shoulders as they approached the camp, she closed her eyes against what she knew would be prying eyes and interested gazes. If she did not see it, she could merely pretend that it wasn't happening, she reasoned.

Finally, Hoskuld leaned forward, taking them through the opening to their tent and she could open her eyes once more. The darkness of the room was exactly what she needed.

She had never done this before. Sure, she had fondled and played around with boys and, even older men. But that had been childish games as she was innocently awakened to being a woman. Now, it was the real thing, the true becoming of adulthood. Melkorka relished the notion that she would later leave this tent as a different person, as one that had been ravished thoroughly and she leaned in to kiss Hoskuld with such ferocity that he chuckled at her.

"I do believe that you want me," he whispered into her ear as he laid her down in the furs. His hot breath tickled across her neck and sent shivers down her back.

She bit her lip as his body towered over hers and the weight of him blanketed her body. His face came closer and he also nibbled gently at her lip. Melkorka gasped in response. She melted into him as his bite turned into a kiss.

He leaned on one arm as they embraced. His body still covered her but his weight was off to one side, giving his other hand the freedom to explore. Hoskuld's fingers ran over her hip, climbing higher until they touched the swell of her breast. He paused and she opened her eyes.

Staring at her, as though questioning, she allowed her hands to roam in response. They trailed over his chest and he resumed his own exploration. Covering her breast, she felt the heat of his touch through her clothing. Her nipples hardened and she groaned once more.

"That's right," Hoskuld whispered hoarsely into her ear. "I want to hear just how much you want me."

She swallowed hard as his tongue darted out and trickled its way from her ear and down her neck. Her skin was on fire with his touch and she reached up, squeezing his shoulders and grinding into him as she did so.

"That's it," he said and kissed lower still.

He pulled away and Melkorka felt her whole world dissolve as he did so. Sitting up, he quickly pulled his tunic over his head. Then his shirt was removed and Melkorka sat up as well.

She needed to touch him, to feel the skin and muscle of him. His skin was warm, hot to the touch as she raked her fingers up his chest. She wanted to feel all of him, to know every single part of this man and she leaned in, resting her forehead against his chest as she listened to his heartbeat. Hoskuld wrapped his arm around her and she had never felt so secure in all of her life.

He ran his fingers down her arms and they crossed over to her stomach as they pried at the edges of her tunic. She allowed him to do so and reached down, also grabbing at the edges and lifting the item of clothing up and over her head. His fingers trailed along behind, running briefly over her nipples as he did so.

She shuddered at the action and when he reached her shoulders, he pushed her back down again. Melkorka settled into the furs as he reached lower, grabbing at her undershirt and raking it along her calves, up over her knees, her thighs, and she shivered as the cool air rushed over her hot skin.

Closing her eyes, she groaned in response as Hoskuld kissed her thighs. His lips trailed higher and Melkorka felt alive as a fire raged through her body. Reaching closer to her core, she panted out her desire for his touch. His fingers clasped her hips, pulling her towards him and her knees parted involuntarily with the action.

He dove in. Touching her coarse hair, his tongue darting out in response. Reaching down, her fingers twined in his braids and she felt him push in further, kissing her down there as he had earlier on her lips.

Melkorka let out a hoarse grunt of desire and Hoskuld raised his head. Moving upwards, he continued to tug at her clothing, exposing her stomach, her chest. She watched him watching her. His desire was akin to a wild animal singling in on its prey and her insides clenched hard in response. Melkorka wanted to scream, to call out his name, to tell him that she wanted him to take her now.

But, she did none of those things. Instead, she threw her head back, her fingers tangling in his hair and pulling him towards her.

Hoskuld dived in, kissing her nipple and trailing his wet touch up to her neck, nipping gently at her skin as he went and she felt the intensity of it rushing through her, igniting her and making the dampness increase between her legs.

He suckled at one nipple as he continued to pull her clothes over her head. She was now naked before him and she felt vulnerable. Yet, at the same time, it was as though this was the one place in which she had been travelling to for her entire life. Somehow, this was where she belonged and she never wanted to be parted from the man who was towering over her.

His lips reached hers and she could taste her own juices as his tongue darted out. Leaning into the kiss, she wrapped her arms around his shoulders and pulled him into her. She couldn't get close enough to him as their embrace intensified.

"I want you," Hoskuld said and she opened her eyes. He

gazed at her with such wanton desire that she could feel her emotion welling up, ready to spill over. Leaning in, he kissed the corner of one eye and her tears did finally fall. "I will never hurt you."

In that moment, she believed him. She wanted nothing more than to become a part of his life, to travel to his homeland and settle into a new existence. Thoughts of Jorunn were pushed to the side as his fingers reached down and touched her core. A groan roared out of her and she felt as though she were ready to explode.

Stretching up, his body rubbed against hers and her legs twined around his waist as he rushed to lower his pants. She was so ready for him that she couldn't wait a moment longer.

As soon as he was completely naked, she pulled him into her, his chest crashing against her as her fingernails dug into his back. Reaching down, his hand guided himself into her and she felt the warmth of it against her thigh a moment before it nudged at her opening.

Resistance met him as he gently pushed against her. There was a blinding heat, a flash of pain, and then he was inside of her and her entire world shrunk down to this single moment in time.

Carefully, he moved against her, gauging her reaction and she dug her nails in further to encourage him. Melkorka felt the enormity of him as he did so and she wondered at how she could take him all. Yet, her body accommodated and he paused as soon as he had sunk as far as he could go.

He pulled back and plunged in once more. Her legs wrapped further around him and she allowed his pace as she felt her own desire growing. His thrusts continued until, finally, she felt his need eclipsing her own and he cried out. Her own tension built as he did so and his single groan, erupting long and deep, was enough to tip her over the edge along with him.

CHAPTER 12: HOSKULD

HOSKULD WOKE WITH THE WEIGHT OF THE woman's head on his chest. One arm stretched out over him and he reached down to take hold of her delicate fingers. He was sated, so much so that he wondered if what he and Jorunn had shared previously had really happened. He had never felt this way with his wife. And, she had never encouraged him as this woman did. Instead, Jorunn allowed his passion and then laid there as she waited for it to be over, a hesitant passenger on a reluctant journey.

Even without words, this woman had shown him more desire. Hoskuld kissed the top of her head and she roused slightly. He held his breath until she settled back into sleep again.

"I will always protect you," he whispered into her hair as his fingers trailed gently down her back.

While he did not want to disturb her slumber, he was also eager to find out if she still wanted him this morning. Perhaps she would wake up and realise her mistake. Or, maybe she had not felt the same he had during their night of passion. He hoped this was not so, his heart sinking with the thought.

Hoskuld would do everything he could to make this woman happy. He did not want her to look on him as Jorunn did.

They were content within their union, happy at times. However, Jorunn had never really wanted him. Even when he approached her father with the notion of marriage, she had said that she would agree to it only if her father did.

While not a rejection, it was near close to it. If Hoskuld had not been as wealthy as he was, her father could have just as easily dismissed the proposal. Jorunn would have likely been happier with that agreement.

She had been a beauty when Hoskuld had first laid eyes on her. Many men were vying for her affection and she was standoffish with all of them. Hoskuld had decided to ask her father regardless as no one else had been ambitious enough to do so. Her beauty aroused desire but she was also intimidating to the young men.

It had likely been his forwardness in this regard that made her consider the proposal and her father to agree to it. Perhaps he should have let her be. Their union had been loveless and it made neither of them happy.

Although, he could no longer imagine his life without their young children. It was a terrible mess of confusion when he thought about the whole situation. Maybe this woman would help fill the void that Jorunn had created in him. And, it would free her up from her obligations towards him.

He tried to remember if he had ever seen his wife interested in anyone outside of their marriage but came up blank. The only person Jorunn seemed to spend more time with, other than her children, was her lifelong friend, Otta. If she was disappointed over their union because she loved someone else, she had done a very good job of hiding it over the years.

The woman stirred once more, rolling over and exposing her breast for a moment before she pulled the furs up. Her nipple was hard against the cold of the morning and he wished to rub his thumb over it but he heard activity outside.

Everyone was rising, ready to be on the move again. His longship was loaded and ready to go. Soon they would cross the sea and return home. He ached for Iceland, for the open vistas and the familiarity of it.

He kissed the woman's head once more. "Time to awaken my sleeping beauty."

She stirred, one arm stretching up as she groaned into the morning. The furs dropped back and her breasts were exposed once more. Leaning down, he kissed one nipple and watched her eyes flash open, her pupils dilate and a startled expression crossed her face only briefly before she smiled at him. Reaching down, she cupped his chin.

To Hel with what was going on outside, they could all wait, and Hoskuld dived in for another kiss. This quickly turned to more sensual activities and they ended up having a late start to their travels.

THE OPEN SEA SPREAD out in front of them and Hoskuld wrapped his arms around the woman as she leaned against him. So far, the voyage had been smooth and she appeared to have settled into travelling, not getting sick as she had on the last trip.

"Iceland has volcanoes," Hoskuld said. "Have you heard

of them?"

She shook her head in response.

"They are like giant hills that sometimes shudder and spew forth hot liquid that settles over the land and hardens to rock afterward. They can be dangerous if you are close by but spectacular to watch from a distance. They are wild, uncontrollable."

The woman nodded as she listened to him.

"It is beautiful, though, and much wilder than what you see here in Norway, or in your own country, I suppose. There are not so many people and we are spread out. There is plenty of solitude, so I hope that you enjoy that."

She nodded once more and Hoskuld brushed her hair out of the way before kissing her cheek.

"We have plenty of gatherings if you do need to see people, though," he added. "But, mostly, we are farmers and spend our days tending to our livestock or crops. I used to travel once every two years to serve with King Haakon and, even though he says that he will not likely serve for much longer, if he does, I should like to take you with me when I travel there next. Jorunn was never interested in doing so and I think she enjoyed the break from me."

Hoskuld was silent then. He turned his gaze out to the open sea once more and searched for his homeland, even though he knew that it was far too early to lay sights on it yet. In fact, they would see the Faroe Islands on their larboard side well before they saw Iceland.

His thoughts turned, once more, to how Jorunn would react when he returned home. He could see no reason why she should be upset but, deep inside, he knew that she would be so, especially with the terms on which they had departed.

Not only did Jorunn like control and he had taken that from her decisively, but it was also a slap in the face regarding their argument before he left.

"Regardless of how my wife reacts when we arrive home," he said. "Always remember that I care deeply for you, that I will do everything within my power to make your life happy. There is no reason for Jorunn to be against what I have done but she is a complicated woman and, even though she doesn't really desire me, she may also be jealous of you. After all, she has long been considered the most attractive woman in Iceland. In fact, before I laid eyes on you, I believed that no other woman could surpass her regarding looks. But you certainly do. And, that may unsettle her above all other reasoning."

The woman turned and looked up at him. He couldn't fathom what she was thinking, whether she believed his words or if she was worried about meeting Jorunn. However, when she leaned in to kiss him, he understood her desire. And, that was all that mattered to him now.

"I am so lucky to have found you," he said. "Do you believe that fate brings people together?"

The woman nodded at him as she leaned into his chest. He held her tight, protecting her from the wind now whipping up around them.

"Our kind believe that everything is preordained. So, our meeting was always going to happen and there is no way in which either of us could change it. I am thankful for that knowledge, for knowing that the gods want this to happen, that they have worked tirelessly to make sure that we met. So, I will do everything within my powers to keep the gods happy regarding our union."

The woman trembled under his touch and he wondered if

it was because of the cold creeping in or at his words. He honestly believed everything that he had just told her and there was nothing that would stop him from making sure that they always rang true.

CHAPTER 13: MELKORKA

MELKORKA HAD FINALLY FOUND HER SEA legs. She was happy to sit on the edge of the longship, watching the waves as they crashed along the sides of the wooden vessel, even in inclement weather.

In fact, she now loved watching the water as she leaned far out over the edge of the vessel. Hoskuld had taught her the parts of the ship and explained how the ropes and sails worked. She took in all of the information, excited to be learning something entirely new.

If she were to be a part of his life and, if she were to travel with him in the future, she needed to know these things. But, more than that, she wanted to know everything about him. If he was interested in something, then so was she.

Never in her wildest dreams would she have been able to learn such things or to be introduced to them. Melkorka hugged herself tightly as she watched the land approach. No, her life had struck out entirely different from what she had imagined while growing up in Eriu. She couldn't believe just how excited she was to be exactly where she was right now.

Even if they were fast approaching Hoskuld's homeland

where a wife already waited for him.

Melkorka wondered at how their first meeting would go. Would Jorunn be excited at Hoskuld's return? Would she rush at him and throw her arms around his neck, kissing him and suggesting they be alone for a while?

From what Hoskuld had said about his wife, that would not happen. She was reserved around him and had never really enjoyed their intimate company. Not like Melkorka did, anyway.

She blushed at the thought. They had been together a lot during the voyage. Melkorka was voracious when it came to knowing him in such a manner and she no longer cared what the others thought as they captured quiet moments aside from the main group.

Little had she known that she would be that interested in laying with a man. Previously, growing up, she had not really thought much about what people did within the marital bed beyond knowing that it happened. She had not pursued the idea as many women of her age had.

In fact, it seemed to be all that they wanted to talk about. When it would happen, how, and with whom. Melkorka had kept out of these conversations, thinking that sex was not anything more important other than a means by which to have children.

Now, though, she suddenly understood the mass appeal of it. She knew why men were always sidling up to women, making lewd comments and gestures in order to attempt to woo them, and why women allowed it.

Melkorka couldn't understand why Jorunn wasn't interested in Hoskuld. He was attentive and affectionate as well as being proudly aggressive when required. Or, perhaps Hoskuld was underestimating Jorunn's reaction to him.

She tried not to dwell on this idea too often. As her hand reached out to trail through the icy water, Melkorka forced herself to consider the fact that Hoskuld had been lying all along and that he had just been lonely when he bought her.

Shuddering against the cold water over her fingers, she thought about how she would feel if she were Jorunn and Hoskuld arrived home with a new woman in tow. She would be livid.

However, she had heard the others onboard talk of Jorunn and they seemed to back up what Hoskuld said about her. Even Birgir seemed to know of Jorunn's personality. She was often described as beautiful but cold or distant and she hoped this was the case. She would hate to ruin a woman's life like that.

A hand on her shoulder made her realise that Hoskuld had arrived and she turned, smiling up at him. She patted the spot next to her and Hoskuld sat down.

Melkorka turned back to the approaching land which was already filling her view entirely. She was scared as she saw the tall peaks of what Hoskuld called "volcanoes" starting to reveal themselves. The land already looked foreign and strange because of these great formations.

The shadow of clouds covered the sun briefly and she shivered in response, wondering if it was an omen as to what would happen once she arrived in Iceland. Would it be a desolate place filled with nothing but a woman who would resent her? Turning to Hoskuld once more, her gaze searching his, questioning, and she hoped he understood the implication.

He reached out, clasping her hand and squeezing it gently. "Everything will be alright, dear woman. You just have to trust me on that."

Melkorka blinked at him, hoping that this was the case. She trusted him, for sure. However, Jorunn was an unknown element. There was nothing to judge her by other than the stories told by those around her. Until she laid eyes on the woman and could make up her own mind on the matter, she would continue to fret.

She watched as the land approached and details came into focus. First, the volcanoes, tall, ominous, strangely proud as they dominated the landscape. Then, as they got closer, grey gave way to the white of ice and, finally, to the green of the land. She could see the occasional tree but the land was much more barren than she was used to. Melkorka was unsure how she would cope without all the leafy coverage that trees provided. The landscape made her feel vulnerable, as though she was as exposed as it was and she would be judged accordingly.

She could see the black edges of this new world, bleaching out to the grey of pebbles as they got closer to the water's edge. It was a strange place. Hauntingly beautiful, though, and Melkorka could feel the rise of excitement at the prospect of having a new place to explore. She had loved her time alone in Norway, searching the countryside.

Even if she had an ulterior motive at the time, and was hoping to find people that could help her escape her confinement, there had been another emotion under the surface. The forest calmed her. Being among the foliage was relaxing and she had relished wandering alone for all those days.

Melkorka hoped that she would be able to explore this new landscape, that she could find the comforting blanket of trees that she so desperately needed. Everything would be alright if only she could find the familiar cover of the woodlands.

The longship grated against the pebbly bottom as they struck land and Melkorka lurched forward. Hoskuld grabbed at her briefly before jumping overboard and dropping to his knees. She watched as he leaned over, clasping the pebbles in his hands and kissing the ground.

"I have missed you, Iceland," he said before rising and putting a hand out to help Melkorka off the ship.

His hands still had a catchment of pebbles as she reached out to him. It was her first touch of his homeland and she clasped tightly at his hands, crushing the hard rocks between them. The dull pain was somehow a comfort.

"You are home now," Hoskuld said to her and Melkorka truly hoped this strange new land welcomed her as much as he did.

CHAPTER 14: JORUNN

AS SOON AS THE APPEARANCE OF THE longship was noticed, people had been rushing to the shore all day long. Jorunn hung back, though. She missed her husband but was also relieved when he was away from home.

It wasn't that she hated him. She just didn't really have any feelings in particular for Hoskuld. He was a good match; their union had been based on that and she was always thankful that he had been kind to her over the years even though she was not easy to live with.

Plus, there was the fact that they had argued before Hoskuld left.

It made her wonder where they now stood once he returned. She had said some horrible things to him, and he in return. Jorunn had mulled over their argument heavily while Hoskuld was gone and had yet to come to a decision regarding their future. He was her husband and a good man. Yet, she didn't love him and never had.

It had been hard while he was gone, with three young children to raise. However, the community got behind her and helped out as much as they could. Otta had helped her. They were all more her family than her husband. Although he was attentive and provided well for her, she felt no connection to him like she did with those who were always there and who always had her back when it came to everyday life.

She couldn't resent Hoskuld for his actions, it was the way of their people, after all. Plus, to spend time with King Haakon was certainly an obligation one never turned down. It gave her freedom away from him.

"Is that papa's ship?" Thorleik asked and Jorunn looked down upon her young son. She ruffled his hair and smiled at him. Jorunn may not have a deep love for her husband but she would never allow her children to realise that. Or hadn't, until their argument.

"I think it is. I suppose you are most excited to see him after all of this time has passed?"

Thorleik nodded at her before darting off. She could hear him yelling out about the imminent arrival and Jorunn could at least be excited on his behalf.

Standing on top of the bank and looking down over the beach, Jorunn watched the approaching vessel. She would smile and welcome Hoskuld home, even allowing him to lean in and kiss her cheek if he approached. Still, she didn't like the outward show of affection. She never had, not just between her and her husband but, with people in general. The only exception to that rule was with her children, of whom she kissed regularly.

Jorunn wondered at the voyage and of how they had travelled. She had spoken openly of wishing for bad weather during their last argument and she wondered if the gods had listened to her.

There were always scrapes and near-misses that made her frightened for the safety of them all. They would relish telling her, of scaring her and she bit down on her lip, as though bracing herself against the onslaught she knew would follow once they touched down on the shore, hoping that her words had not caused any extra calamity.

✝

WHEN THE SHIP FINALLY scraped against solid ground, Jorunn was already wondering why the woman was on board. Hoskuld stood next to her and dread settled down upon Jorunn's shoulders.

Perhaps this was punishment for her harsh words. Hoskuld was not normally spiteful but even she knew that she had gone over the edge regarding their argument.

Yet, a part of her was relieved. She had always wondered when Hoskuld would take on a concubine. Now that they had four children, she felt no need to actively encourage her husband into their bed of a night time. Jorunn had plenty to do regarding her offspring and did not feel the need for marital duties.

However, she felt sorry for Hoskuld, who was voracious if encouraged. Yet, he always listened to her and turned over when she brushed him aside. Sometimes, she had remained awake until Hoskuld finally fell asleep and noticed just how long it took for him to wind down afterward without her release.

For that, she always felt bad.

Yet, she was harried, exhausted at the end of each day. Without any real love for Hoskuld, something she had tried to fake at the start but had never really grown into over time, she never felt the desire to lay with him, to enjoy his company just for the sake of it.

Jorunn wondered what it was like to truly love someone, to want to reach out and touch them as she saw plenty of other couples do, even in broad daylight and in front of other people. Sometimes she ached for that sort of relationship with Hoskuld. But she also knew, deep down inside, that she would never love him in the way he wanted. She just didn't have it in her and it wasn't just him, it was men in general.

Still, there was a certain pride to be gained by not loving as others did. Love only complicated things, it gave the other person a means to control. Jorunn liked being her own person and loving her children was more than enough vulnerability for her.

"Jorunn," Hoskuld said as he climbed the bank. "It has been some time, hasn't it?"

He hugged her awkwardly before pulling away again. She didn't know whether to be relieved or upset that he had forsaken even the small measure of affection they had between them.

"Who is this?" she asked, not even waiting for a quiet moment to question him like she normally would as the memory of their previous argument swelled in her mind.

"Would you believe me if I told you that I don't know her name?"

The woman stepped forward, leaning into Hoskuld and staring at Jorunn with impossibly green eyes. Jorunn had never seen such beauty in a woman, even without the mark of foreign appeal strong on her.

Hoskuld put an arm around the woman's shoulders and the intimacy between them was evident for everyone surrounding them. Jorunn fought hard not to shirk away.

"That makes no sense," Jorunn replied. "You obviously know this woman well, how can you not even ask her what her name is?"

"I know it seems strange," Hoskuld said, untangling himself from the woman and Jorunn saw a brief frown cross the foreigner's face. Somehow, it made her feel infinitely better about the situation. This woman loved her husband, that was obvious. "She does not speak. The man I bought her from said that she is a mute but I know that she understands quite well."

Jorunn nodded at her husband, trying to hide her incredulousness as their children darted around her and threw themselves at their father. She smiled at how happy they were to see him but her joy was tainted by her own strange feeling of jealousy towards Hoskuld's new woman and their tentative relationship. For some strange reason, she wanted nothing more than to ruin his happiness in the way he had just publicly done so to her.

For all that she didn't want Hoskuld, she had only just worked out that she didn't want anyone else to want him either. Her pettiness settled down on her and the uneasiness of it made her stomach squirm.

†

"HOW WAS THE MEETING with King Haakon?" Jorunn asked.

The banquet to welcome her husband home was well underway. Their children had finally succumbed to the tiredness that they had been fighting all day. Jorunn had only put them down to sleep and was now ready to confront her husband about his time away. It was a moment she didn't want to have in front of their children.

"It went well, he wanted me to stay much longer. However, I wanted to get the timber home so that we could start building immediately. Haakon tried to persuade me but seem happy to allow me to return to him at a later date."

"That is why I am here," a drunken Birgir said, leaning across Hoskuld.

Jorunn glared at the man, who she had only just met. She suspected he had many good stories to tell the king about Hoskuld and herself so tried to cover up her irritation with a brittle smile.

"Haakon offered that I come once the building works are complete but he also fears that this was our last visit together," Hoskuld continued, oblivious to Birgir. "Not that he seems particularly feeble so I wonder if there is some plot that he has not made me aware of. Or, perhaps it is just the paranoia of a king who has reigned for such a long time."

Birgir stood, wavering as he did so. Putting a hand on Hoskuld's shoulder for support, he turned to them and bowed.

"I must piss," he said before staggering off across the room.

"Now, tell me more about this woman," Jorunn said as soon as Birgir was swallowed up by the rowdy crowd.

The woman in question was sitting on the other side of Hoskuld and Jorunn watched her closely as she spoke. When the woman stiffened with her words, she knew Hoskuld had, at least, been telling the truth about her intelligence.

"I bought her as a thrall. I think she will be helpful on the farmstead, for all of us."

Hoskuld turned and stared directly at her when he said that. Jorunn frowned at him before turning away, unable to bear the honesty in his words. He was right and, as usual, was actually trying to help her out. So, why did she resent the new situation so much?

"Yet, you didn't consult me," she whispered.

"How could I?" Hoskuld asked. His hand reached out and took her chin, turning her back towards him. She looked down at her cup rather than make eye contact. "And, why should I?"

Jorunn looked up at those words. Hoskuld's blue-eyed gaze bore into her and she thought—for the first time—that she could see how someone would love this man. He was handsome, of that she had no doubt. She had just never felt any raging passion for him. Now, she wondered if she actually could.

"Because I am your wife," she hissed through tense lips.

"Are you jealous, my dear?" Hoskuld asked.

For the first time she could hear the bitterness in his words. Jorunn had damaged him, left him hanging for way too long and now she was about to reap exactly what she had sown over the season of their loveless marriage.

He still held her chin and she slapped his hand out of the

way as she leaned back into her chair.

"Of course, I'm not," Jorunn lied. "Why should I be envious of some poor thrall that has no choice in what happens to her. If that is how you want to live your life then I certainly will not tell you otherwise. However, do not expect me to treat her with any great favour on your behalf."

Her words were hollow and she feared that Hoskuld was aware of it. He always knew her better than she knew herself.

"She is supposed to be of a royal bloodline, so I will not allow her to be treated like a common thrall."

Jorunn recoiled at his words.

"You have been taken for a fool then, husband." She spat that last word out before she turned to him. "I will not suffer a fool under my roof or a thrall who pretends that they are more than they actually are. If I mean anything to you, then you cannot lie with her while we still share the same house. You need to get it out of your mind that she is more important than your wife."

Jorunn rose and stormed out of the room, knocking into Birgir as he returned and not even caring about how he would report back to the king. She would not be told that a beautiful foreign thrall had more status than herself, not within her own marriage.

Even if she didn't love Hoskuld.

CHAPTER 15: MELKORKA

AS SOON AS SHE SAW JORUNN SHE KNEW WITH a devastating blow that her life was not to be as she had built it up on their sea voyage. In that first meeting, Jorunn hid it well but she was desolate at her husband's betrayal.

Hoskuld may have believed that there was no love between them but Jorunn felt something. Whether it was love or just the familiarity of having the same person in her life for a long time, Melkorka's presence had been hard on her, regardless.

Melkorka sidled up to Hoskuld as Jorunn approached. He held her hand briefly before stepping forward to greet his wife. The void between them afterward had continued to crack open further. The cold of rejection flowed in and the realisation of her true fate—that of a slave—took the place of the fanciful world she had created in her head.

What a fool she had been to think that she and Hoskuld would live as husband and wife, that Jorunn would be alright with the arrangement.

Later that night, it had gotten worse.

In front of everyone, Jorunn had said, on absolutely no uncertain terms that Hoskuld was to sleep with his wife, and her alone. There was no room for Melkorka in Jorunn's world and she wondered what would happen next.

Gazing up at the stars as Hoskuld led her to her new quarters, Melkorka breathed in the cold night air, amazed at its purity, at the dense thickness of it as it filled her lungs with the cold crispness of it. This place was beautiful, cold, distant, just like Jorunn herself.

"I will be back in the morning and we will talk. Or, I will. I hope that you listen," Hoskuld said.

Turning to her, he wrapped his arms around her and Melkorka felt frozen in his embrace. She wanted to respond, to feel the heat of his touch again but her pride held her back.

This was never going to work. She had no choice but to believe that now. All the words that Hoskuld had spoken upon their first meeting and up until this point in time had been naught but pretty lies wrapped up in an embroidered linen and given to her like a fanciful gift. She had seen nothing but the beautiful material of it, the engaging prettiness and believed everything he said without consequence. Now, she was stuck here, falling in love with a man who was already taken, one who had always been owned by someone else.

"I want you to believe that what I have said about my wife, still stands. Her reaction tonight is only her jealousy at you, not her true feelings for me."

Melkorka rested her head against Hoskuld's chest and felt the hammering of his heart. Finally, she wrapped her arms around his waist and allowed herself this single luxury. His words may have mirrored her thoughts somewhat but she didn't think it would change a single thing. Pulling away from him, Melkorka turned and entered the sparse room that was her new home. She didn't look back and Hoskuld said nothing more. As soon as his footfalls could no longer be heard, she crumpled to the ground and cried.

"GOOD MORNING," HOSKULD SAID and Melkorka smiled before she had a chance to remember the day before. She was weary, oh so weary, from the emotional upheaval of everything. Yet, for a brief moment in time, she saw Hoskuld's face smiling at her and she could pretend that they were on his ship, that the waves were lapping against the sides of his boat and they were happy.

"I hope that you slept well," he said and the memories started flooding in.

Looking around, Melkorka noted the wooden walls, roughly hewed, as though she had been placed in a barn stall and not the main house. She wondered what this room had been for prior to her arrival. Perhaps it was for animals. Her heart sunk and she frowned at Hoskuld before sitting up.

He led her out to the main room, the one that his family spent a lot of their time in. It was vastly different, yet, also incredibly similar to her own home in Eriu. The sudden memory of her nanny bringing her tea crippled her with grief. She forced the thought from her mind before others crept in, memories more defeating like those of her father.

Standing, she stoked at the dying embers of the fire and started a kettle of water to heat. Her actions were to distract herself against what was about to come.

The room was empty and Melkorka was thankful for that. Although, she suspected Hoskuld had sent everyone away so that he could talk to her and she felt obligated to listen to him now. The rejection in the room was so close that she could taste it like the thick smoke starting to coil around the kettle in front of her.

"We need to talk," Hoskuld said, his tone quiet but also commanding.

Reaching up, he took her hands, encouraging her to sit down beside him. Melkorka did it but only because she wanted the moment to be over. Let him break it to her gently so that she could go back to trying to work out what came next in her strange new life.

"I have spoken again to my wife and let her know that I cannot, that I will not, cast you aside. She is still jealous but I think that she is in agreeance that our marriage is not a happy one."

Melkorka looked at him with confusion. She was waiting for his words to change, for him to tell her that she was no longer his shiny new thing but what he had said instilled a small glimmer of hope in her heart.

Had Hoskuld actually defended her?

She didn't know how to feel about that. If she were Jorunn, she would be devastated at the arrival of a new woman to take over from her. Yet, what if she really didn't love him? What if she was just embarrassed that Hoskuld had confronted her like that and made it so obvious that they had failings within the marriage. Yes, she could see how that would upset the woman.

"While Jorunn is not happy at your arrival, she can also see the advantage of the situation. We have been loveless for so long that this will be a welcome event for her eventually, she just needs some time to get used to it. She has admitted that she is glad that she no longer has to welcome me if she doesn't want it."

Melkorka wondered when this conversation had occurred. The farmstead was solid but, as with any house, sounds always permeated through the walls and conversations could often be heard, even those in hushed tones. Hoskuld continued to talk, even as she was distracted.

"...Jorunn is happy with our marriage otherwise and wants to maintain that, even if we are not truly together anymore. She wants the children to think that we are happy and that our marriage is strong."

Hoskuld paused and Melkorka watched him closely, trying to work out if he spoke the truth. He smiled at her before continuing.

"And, it is, mostly. We can get along outside of it all and can happily work together regarding our family and our homestead. I want it to continue and so does she."

Hoskuld leaned in, his fingers reaching out for her, searching. Melkorka pulled away in response. It was an instinct that she didn't fight against.

"I understand that you are mad with me," Hoskuld said, settling back into his seated position once more. "I will not force you. I have never wanted to do that and you know it."

His eyes implored her and Melkorka could feel herself melting under his gaze. He would always do that to her, make her want him even though she shouldn't.

"Please, understand that I never expected Jorunn to act this way when we returned. Her reaction has surprised me and I think we need to give her time to process the situation. However, I do not want to end things with you, of which Jorunn is well aware. I have made it very clear that I will continue my relationship with you if that is what you still want."

His gaze intensified with those words and Melkorka could sense the question there. Hoskuld wanted her to accept him, to allow this to happen, to free him of the guilt he was now feeling. Yet, she couldn't do that. Melkorka was angry at what had happened last night. Jorunn had made her feel like property once again and it was a feeling that Hoskuld had washed away with his love for her. She did not want to be simply property. She couldn't be, she was a princess, after all.

"I have a proposal," Hoskuld finally said. "I hope it will placate you."

Once again, his words stroked her emotions and she wanted him to satisfy her but not in the way he was proposing.

"Jorunn has agreed that you can stay, that we can continue if you will allow it. However, she does not want to see evidence of it. She doesn't want our love to be pushed into her face and be on display for all to see. I am not happy with that but I think, over time, she will soften to this arrangement."

Melkorka was so confused. She wanted Hoskuld. Even after everything, she wanted him so badly. Yet, she was also embarrassed to be treated in this way. Did she really want to lower herself to being nothing more than a dirty hidden secret?

Her hand trembled as she reached out. Her nails scraped against Hoskuld's face and pushed aside his braids. She watched as he leaned into her touch and closed his eyes. She rested her forehead against his, also closing her eyes and hot tears that had been welling finally fell, spilling down her cheeks.

Hoskuld wiped away her tears. His lips searched hungrily for hers. As they crashed against her own, she found that she could not contest the tidal wave of emotion washing over her. Melkorka wanted to fight it, to pull away and punish Hoskuld. Yet, at the same time, her body betrayed her as she kissed him back.

CHAPTER 16: HOSKULD

HOSKULD AWOKE TO THE NOISES OF FAMILY life. He could hear the girls helping with Jorunn, giggling as they did so. Thurid, his youngest child, was crying softly but was silenced quickly as suckling sounds started and Hoskuld knew that the breast had been offered. He had missed awaking to this so much while he was gone across the seas.

They were also hollow sounds now. Jorunn was mad at him, even though a tentative compromise had been met. He knew there would be a transition period when he returned with the new woman. Yet, he thought it would be over quickly. After all, concubine thralls were common. There was no need for Jorunn to feel shame at his new acquisition.

However, he suspected it had less to do with shame and more to do with the loss of control. His wife was a strong woman, a fine one, in fact. Jorunn led their household with expertise and was a credit to their family. She was strict but fair with the children and they would grow up to be wonderful and resilient adults because of this.

"Come eat," Hallgerd called out and Hoskuld smiled at his daughter. She was only three and her words were disjointed, not quite fully formed yet.

"Is it my favourite?" Hoskuld asked as he sat up and threw

the covers back. Jorunn was sitting across from the fire, Thurid still attached to her breast. She smiled down at her child and Hoskuld softened towards her. Regardless of her attitude towards him, Jorunn was a good mother. He must make sure that he treated her as such. Hoskuld may not fully understand why she was mad at him but that was no reason to be angry in return.

"Stew, papa," Hallgerd said as he ruffled her hair.

"Mmmm," he said before leaning over and kissing his wife's head. She did not respond.

Thurid, on the other hand, pulled away from the breast and looked at him, raising a fist as she did so. Hoskuld reached out, allowing the child to wrap her tiny fingers around his forefinger.

"I have missed you all," he said and Jorunn snorted at him.

She would not speak ill while the children were present but he knew that the words were there, ready to be spoken as soon as the chance was offered. He made sure to hurry his breakfast down and leave before she had the opportunity this morning.

"Shall we check the animals, Thorleik?"

Thorleik was their eldest child and eager to learn the ways of their farm. He pulled on his boots as he hurried to follow Hoskuld out the door.

"THIS ONE WILL LIKELY give birth before the week is out," Hoskuld explained as he patted the rump of the animal.

Thorleik had been attentive the entire time, obviously missing having his father around. Hoskuld wondered if he was old enough to travel with him. He would be seven soon and by the next time the meeting of kings came around, he would be almost ten. That was certainly old enough.

Although, Jorunn might object somewhat. Still, there was plenty of time yet to prepare her for this.

"Thorleik has missed you," Olaf said and Hoskuld turned.

His uncle stepped forward, arms outstretched and Hoskuld clapped the man on the back as they embraced.

"It felt like a long time without my children," he replied, smiling down at Thorleik, who beamed proudly.

"It always does when you are away from family." Olaf Feilan stepped in beside him and they started the walk back to the farmhouse. "I hear you bought more than timber with you."

As he spoke, Hoskuld looked towards his home. Already, Thord and Einar were prepping the wood, ready for the expansion. He looked over the huge expanse of wood selected. They had taken much more than they needed but it would likely be useful at some point in time.

"Yes, and I fear that Jorunn is not impressed with me now."

"When was your wife ever impressed with you?" Olaf laughed which turned into a cough. He paused for breath. Hoskuld waited as Olaf rested and he suddenly realised just how old his uncle was getting. King Haakon may think that he was an old man but he was certainly younger than Olaf.

Thorleik had run on ahead, not interested in the talk of adults. Hoskuld watched as his son topped the incline and started the descent down towards their home, disappearing until they topped the ridge as well.

"I am sorry that your marriage has never been entirely happy."

"So am I, Uncle," he replied.

"I also hear that this new woman is of high breeding."

"So says the trader I bought her off. I believe him, though. The woman may not speak but she holds herself as a noblewoman does. Her mannerisms show the true person behind her current position."

Olaf nodded at him. "Is she mute? Perhaps that is why her

family sold her?"

"I don't think so, on either count. I believe that she was captured in Eriu, although I cannot confirm that is where she is from, only that she wears the clothing from there."

"Do you think she will ever talk?"

"If she hasn't now, I doubt she ever will. She is very competent in understanding, so I guess that there is no need for her to do so if she doesn't wish for it."

They had reached the house and the sound of wood being chopped was loud enough that the pair had to raise their voices to speak above it.

"I hope she makes you happy," he said before stepping through the door. "You deserve that."

Olaf had always been supportive of Hoskuld, even as a child. He smiled as he followed his uncle through the door. His children dashed forward, ready to greet him so soon after his departure that it made him feel terrible for being away so long.

"Jorunn, it has been so long," Olaf said as the woman stepped up to greet him.

"It has," she replied. "It is hard, when you have little ones, to visit family as often as you would like, especially when your husband is overseas on important duties."

Hoskuld felt the sting of her words, a compliment wrapped up with a fishing barb on the end.

"It is those important duties that got you the wood that you so desperately required for improvements to our farm," Hoskuld responded, already on edge around her.

"I agree," Olaf said, instantly on his side. "A young man is always away on duties. However, I am here and able to use my own legs, so it is also my fault that I have not journeyed here so often. I will try harder from now on."

Hoskuld watched Jorunn's expression closely. He could see her conflict. She wanted to continue to work down on Hoskuld some more but couldn't now that Olaf had shouldered some of the blame. He smirked as he turned away, hoping that his wife did not see his expression.

As he did so, the new woman entered the room. She had her head bowed and was carrying a pile of clothing.

"Hello," Olaf said as he approached her. She nodded at him before sitting down by the fire. Placing the clothing down, she took one piece and started the task of mending a hole.

"I see what you mean by she doesn't talk," Olaf said as he turned back to Hoskuld. "She appears to be a good worker, though. And, perhaps having one woman in the household that doesn't speak is actually a blessing."

Olaf winked at Jorunn but Hoskuld could see her straighten her spine at the words.

"So far, she hasn't proven herself. I will leave my judgment yet," she replied as she busied herself with the cauldron over the fire.

"She makes funny faces," Hallgerd said. "I like her."

Hoskuld watched as the woman's tongue darted out towards his daughter and she crossed her eyes as well. The child giggled in response before making her own exaggerated face in reply.

Jorunn huffed as she worked and Hoskuld had the notion that she did not like the fact that even her children were favourable towards the new addition to their family.

The woman returned to her task, her back straight as she stitched at the garment.

"I see what you mean about her being highbred," Olaf finally said as Jorunn handed out warm beverages. Hoskuld sipped the hot liquid. He had missed Jorunn's special blend of raudr tea.

"It is merely fancy words spoken at the point of sale," Jorunn interjected. "Every thrall trader says the same thing in order to get a higher price. My husband is a fool for believing it."

"I don't think so," Olaf replied. "Look at her, Jorunn. Take a good look at how she sits, at how she entered the room earlier. That is not newly learned under the instruction of a trader. That is a behaviour learned from the time of a babe. She is highbred, there is no doubt of that in my eyes."

"Then you are as easily swayed as my husband," Jorunn said. She laughed as she spoke, as though trying to make light of what she had just said but Hoskuld knew that she meant every word spoken.

"Regardless, she stays," Hoskuld said and the woman looked up at him.

He smiled, trying to make her respond personally to him but she bobbed her head once more and continued with her work, her hands shaking as she did so.

Hoskuld thought that he had gotten through to her, that they were friendly once more, as they had been while travelling. Now, he was unsure.

As Hoskuld mused over his tea, the woman suddenly stood. She dropped the clothing and rushed out of the door. A moment later, retching could be heard.

"Are you alright?" Thord could be heard saying. The hammering and chopping were now silent.

Jorunn shrieked and turned to point a finger angrily in his direction.

"What is wrong with the woman?" she asked. "See what happens when you bring home thralls you know nothing about? Feeble is what she is. Feeble and lazy."

"Or pregnant," Olaf responded and the light of the room suddenly bleached out from Hoskuld's vision.

CHAPTER 17: MELKORKA

MELKORKA LEANED OVER THE BUCKET AND heaved once more. It had been the same every morning for a fortnight now. Wiping her mouth, she leaned back onto the bed, hoping that the sickness would pass.

She hadn't expected to be with child. When Hoskuld suggested it to her she had shirked at the notion. However, as the days passed and her moon time never arrived, she knew that it was true.

As she placed her hand over her stomach, she imagined that she could feel the slight swell of a new life there. It was probably too early to really see the roundness of a baby but Melkorka believed that her stomach was no longer as flat as it had been. And, considering how hard it had been for her to keep down food recently, there should be no swell there at all.

"Here's some bread," Hallgerd said as she approached.

Melkorka smiled at the girl and took the food. It was old bread, dry and stale, but it was the only thing that didn't make her feel nauseated of late. She broke it into smaller pieces and placed one in her mouth. Hoskuld arrived with a cup of hot tea. She nodded at him, thankful for the liquid and took a small sip to help push the dry bread down.

Jorunn ignored her now. Ever since it became apparent that her husband had gotten her with child, she had withdrawn.

It was wonderful.

Melkorka wasn't even given spiteful looks or snide comments and her life was settling into a much more peaceful existence.

Still, there were troubles between her and Hoskuld. They were entirely of her own creation, though. She hadn't wanted to become a problem, not between herself and Hoskuld or even between him and his wife. With all that had happened since her arrival, she had avoided his attention.

Well, mostly.

There had been stolen moments when her passion bubbled over and she and Hoskuld found secluded places to continue their love affair. Melkorka didn't know how to feel about those times. She knew now that she had strong feelings for Hoskuld but she also felt rejected by him as he tried to appease his wife as well as her.

It was a horrible mess.

As she swallowed the bread and her stomach began to settle, she looked around the room. It was sectioned off from the other beds. She supposed that Jorunn was happy with that. It made her feel so horribly alone, though, as she settled down into her bed and heard the whisperers of others through the curtain that sectioned off her room. Often, she gazed at the small dark gap that was her own glimpse into the other sleeping quarters. She wondered if Hoskuld was looking at her as she did so, unable to see him through the blackness of the separation between curtain and wall.

Now, the curtain was drawn. Hallgerd had pulled the divider back and left it wide open. The act made Melkorka smile. At least Hoskuld's children liked her.

Stepping out of bed, Melkorka made the small distance to the lavatory to dump her waste products before entering the main room.

"Hello!" Thorleik said and Melkorka smiled at him. "Here, sit with me."

Thorleik made room on the bench for her but she held up her dirty container and pointed to the front door. The child nodded and she stepped outside.

The cold wind assaulted her, tugging at her robe and whipping her hair around. Melkorka tucked her hair behind her ears but it still slapped at her face, stinging as it did so. She would need to get the children to braid her hair today. Coming out here, with the landscape was so open, and where the wind buffeted about regularly, she now understood why braided hair was so popular with the Finngaill.

Reaching the small stream that ran behind the longhouse, Melkorka knelt and rinsed out the container that she had spoiled earlier.

"Are you avoiding me?" Hoskuld asked and she turned in surprise, letting out a startled squeal as she did so.

"Not even when we saw Birgir off have you sided with me. I miss your company," Hoskuld said quietly as he stepped towards her. "Sit with me, speak to me."

Melkorka couldn't work out why she continued to maintain her silence. There was simply no need for it. Yet, it continued. Maybe she still felt delicate in this new environment. Or, perhaps she was still trying to control the situation by doing so? Either way, she felt like she simply couldn't talk after all of this time.

Not, that she hadn't tried.

When alone, she had attempted to speak and her voice had rasped in such a way that she wondered if she actually couldn't talk anymore. Was such a thing possible? Could her words simply stop flowing because she hadn't tried in so long?

She smiled at Hoskuld rather than try to cough out a greeting. He sat down on a wooden bench next to the rushing water and beckoned for her.

Melkorka tapped out the container, placing it down upside down next to the stream and made her way towards Hoskuld. Even with her confusion, her body craved him. She had no choice but to comply and it made her angry at times that he had such control over her, that she allowed it in return.

As their fingers touched, a jolt shot through her, as it always did. Pulling her in, Hoskuld made it impossible for her to sit anywhere but on his lap. Sitting there, she enjoyed the warmth of his body as her breath puffed out like mist in front of them.

Hoskuld nuzzled into her hair, his breath hot against her neck. She closed her eyes, allowing the moment to wash over her.

"I have missed you," he said, the whisper of his words dancing across her skin and making her sigh into it. His fingers traced up her arms, lacing over her stomach and coming to rest on her tiny little imagined bump. "We haven't had a chance to talk about this yet."

Melkorka nodded before Hoskuld continued.

"I am glad that you are with child and I hope that you feel

the same way."

She could sense the question there, the expectation of an answer.

Was she excited about it? She didn't know. All she felt at the moment was the constant sick feeling in the pit of her stomach. It was mostly from the morning illness but, in part, it was the situation in general. Also, having a baby made her miss home even more than she could imagine.

Still, she nodded at Hoskuld. It was what he needed at the moment and it wasn't that she didn't want the baby, it was just that she couldn't work out the mess of emotion that came with it.

He closed his eyes with her admission. His fingers reached up, cupping her face and kissing her tenderly. She leaned into him, her lips meeting his and she knew that nothing else mattered beyond this moment.

"I don't want you to think that your child will be unwanted or treated any differently to my children with Jorunn. Even my wife will not be able to resist a baby. So, have no fear regarding her reaction. Jorunn has many faults but babies melt her every single time."

Melkorka stiffened at the mention of Jorunn and more promises that Hoskuld's wife would be accommodating. She sat up, and as she did so, he spun her around entirely, so that their gaze locked.

"I want you so much that I can't sleep. I wish constantly for the days onboard the ship to return, when we just had ourselves to occupy the days ahead," he said.

Melkorka could feel tears welling and a sob escaped before she could rein in her emotions.

"Please, don't be sad," Hoskuld said and Melkorka opened

her mouth to respond. Hoskuld waited patiently, expectation shining in his gaze but Melkorka clamped her lips together and dropped her gaze to her lap.

"I wish that you would talk to me."

Lifting her chin with his forefinger and thumb, Melkorka had no choice but to return to his gaze once more. Her lips trembled as she sought his forgiveness.

"Another time, then," Hoskuld said with a sigh and Melkorka nodded her head as she touched her forehead to his.

CHAPTER 18: JORUNN

JORUNN OPENED HER EYES AND THE realisation of her life flashed before her. She couldn't complain, yet she did.

With the news of the thrall's pregnancy, Jorunn had closed off from the woman, not sure what to make of the situation. In some ways, it felt like grief, that the woman was providing her husband with yet another child. One that he would adore as much as her own.

Even with her lack of love for him, she wanted him to cherish her, for her to be the one thing that was unique to him. So far, she was the only one who could extend his line, for his name and memory to live on in his children. Now, there was another option, another child was coming that could fill that position and, potentially, exceed beyond her own children.

As she dressed, bitter tears welled and she hoped to compose herself, that her frustration would not ebb out during the day. Her only option was to ignore the woman at the moment, to pretend that she didn't exist. Even as her handmaiden helped her dress, she could hear the moment of the woman rising.

"I will have my braids completely redone, Ashildr," she said and sat down.

"But they were only fixed yesterday," the maiden replied.

"I don't care. They will be redone and there is no need to question me."

Jorunn's back stiffened and she wrapped her hands around the baby secured in a satchel across her body. The woman outside had already passed. Jorunn listened intently as her son spoke to her and then the sound of the door as the woman left.

She despised the fact that her children liked this new woman, that they treated her as Jorunn likely should. There was no reason for her discontent regarding the woman. Only that the arrival of the younger and more beautiful woman had awoken a deep resentment inside of her. The added adoration the woman obviously felt for her husband gave further insult to her conflicted emotions.

If she couldn't love her husband, then no one should.

Jorunn sat patiently as Ashildr undid her tight braids, brushed her hair and then, painstakingly, redid them. She gritted her teeth as the woman pulled her hair tightly, making sure that the braids were secured and wouldn't need doing again for several days.

"There, as you requested," Ashildr finally said before moving off across the room to sort out discarded clothing.

Jorunn rose from the bench and made her way outside.

"Mama!" Thorleik said with as much enthusiasm as he had earlier for the new woman.

"My gorgeous boy," Jorunn exclaimed before swinging him up into her arms. "Are we going to do the washing today?"

"Whatever you wish," the boy replied even though she knew that he didn't like helping with this particular task.

"Once I am done, you can head on down to the market and watch the men training if you like? I will need you to collect some baskets from Irpa since we are short now that there is another person here."

"I like her," Thorleik said as he unravelled himself from her embrace and returned to eating his porridge.

"I am glad that you do," Jorunn lied and sat down next to her son. Ashildr ladled out some hot tea. Taking a long sip, Jorunn watched her son eat. The baby tied to her chest started to wriggle and she put down her drink in order to settle Thurid. Making soothing noises, the child soon went back to sleep. "Perhaps I will come into town with you today."

Jorunn suddenly felt the urge to be around other people, to be free of her home and all of the reminders that there was a new person here, one that loved her husband unconditionally.

"I would like that," Thorleik replied excitedly.

THE TOWN OF LAXARDAL was busy by this time of the day. Jorunn liked the noise and bustle of it though. She absently patted at Thurid, who was all eyes as she stared at all the new things around her. Concentrating on the stalls, waving at friends and family and chatting about the weather, Jorunn tried not to think about the new woman at home.

Thorleik skipped ahead. He knew his way around this market better than even she did and he was always joyful after such a trip.

"Jorunn!"

"Otta," she said, turning at the sound of her name and hugging her friend. "It has been such a while."

Thurid was squashed between them. Pulling back, she pulled Otta's braids from her baby's grasp and her friend laughed at the baby.

"For certain," Otta said. "You need to get out more. Especially now, I hear."

Jorunn scowled at her oldest friend. "News always travels so quickly when there is gossip at the root of it."

"Then Hoskuld did not bring home a new concubine?"

"Of course, he did," she replied, turning and marching on towards Irpa's stall. "But I do not want to dwell on it, nor discuss the matter."

Otta laughed as they walked, linking her arm through Jorunn's and not giving in to her request. "Of course, everyone says that she is more beautiful than even you at her age. They say that she is of royal descent and perfect in every regard. I hope that she is covered in warts and squints because her eyesight is bad. Please tell me this is the case."

Jorunn was silent. Her lips pursed together, creating a thin line that caused a pain in her jowl as she clamped her teeth together.

"I wish she was terrible but most of what you say is true. However, I do not believe that she is of royal blood. She does have one apparent fault, though, and cannot speak. Although, in my opinion, this is in my favour as I don't have to listen to her go on about how wonderful my husband is."

Her friend snorted at her comment. They were so close that Jorunn could feel Otta's warm breath tickling her neck as she spoke.

"Well, that is a blessing! Perhaps Hoskuld will tire of her fairly quickly. After all, who wants a woman just for pleasure?"

Jorunn scowled. Had she actually just said that out loud? Turning, she swatted Otta before answering.

"Every man I have ever come across would pick someone that is good in the furs over a great conversationalist. I have no idea where you find your men. Perhaps we need to get out more together. I think that I should rather find one of the men you speak of than what I already have."

"And, maybe that is why your husband has found another?"

"I think that you had better concentrate more on finding yourself a husband and less time on my marriage."

"But I do not require a man, you know that. However, I will honour your request. Shall we talk of your husband's dear uncle then? I hear that he is very sick."

Jorunn nodded.

Hoskuld had spoken of visiting him. She had avoided the conversation as it seemed likely that her husband was also taking his new thrall with him to show off her growing pregnancy. It was something that she didn't really want to share.

"Hoskuld will be visiting him today. I suppose he doesn't have long left in him. He has lived a good life, though. It's a shame that battle did not take him."

Even with all her misgivings about her husband, she still held his family in high esteem.

"Perhaps Odin will look favourably on his past and choose wisely," Otta said.

"Perhaps."

"Mama, hurry," Thorleik called and all the talk of her miserable life was forgotten for a while as she visited with Irpa. Thankfully, the basket weaver had no gossip to impart regarding Jorunn's life and she was grateful for that.

CHAPTER 19: MELKORKA

THE HOUSE SMELLED OF DEATH AS THEY entered and Melkorka rubbed at her belly, hoping that her child was protected from the grim spectre that enveloped them.

"Dear Olaf," Hoskuld said as he sat beside the old man in the bed.

Melkorka sat next to Hoskuld. Her belly was getting so big that she found the need to sit often. The man in the bed was sunken in appearance and the furs appeared to swallow him. She had to look closely to see his breath moving the bed coverings over his chest.

"I am glad to see you once more," Olaf said and Melkorka lowered her eyes. Looking at her hands, she wished that she was anywhere but in this room.

"What are you saying, old man? You are doing just fine. I expect to see you over this illness in a few days."

She smiled bitterly at Hoskuld's words. Melkorka didn't know if he believed them or if he was merely speaking kindness to the dying man. She hoped it was the latter because everyone could see that this man was not long for this world.

Olaf tried to laugh at Hoskuld's words but a wheeze

escaped instead. He coughed once and a handmaiden stepped in to help the man to have a sip of water. Once he recovered, he reached out a pale leathery hand and Hoskuld clasped it firmly.

"Any fool knows that those words are false, Hoskuld. I love you like a son but I do not want you to think that I will be staying here for much longer. I have other places to be and the gods are already gathering to welcome me there."

As the silence lengthened, Melkorka snuck a quick look out from underneath her eyelashes to confirm that Hoskuld was fighting back his emotions rather than speak and betray his true feelings. She reached out and squeezed the fist in his lap.

"Instead of all this talk of my departure, why don't you tell me more about when your new baby is due to be born?" Olaf said, looking directly at Melkorka

Olaf always spoke to her as though she would respond. The way in which he casually included her was almost enough to make her reply to him. However, she was well practised in the art of keeping silent by now and she rubbed her belly instead.

"It is not long, I imagine," Olaf spoke, following on without hesitation when she didn't answer. She was thankful that he always did that rather than try to coax words out of her. "I hope to see your child born but fear that I will not get that privilege. Regardless, I am sure that the gods will notify me when it finally occurs."

Hoskuld was still silent and Melkorka raised her gaze to smile at the old man. He returned a quick grin before closing his eyes and settling back into the furs. They sat there until gentle snores filled the room. Melkorka eventually tugged at Hoskuld's sleeve and they rose to leave.

Once outside, the bright light hurt her eyes and she leaned against Hoskuld for support. She loved the idea of being a mother soon. However, the problems associated with her pregnancy were not a welcome occurrence. She was sick of feeling sick and tired of having to check her balance, or of having itchy skin and the rising burn in her throat after eating. Already, she could feel the need to relieve herself once more and she pulled once more on Hoskuld's sleeve to alert him.

"What is it now?" Hoskuld asked and she detected a hint of annoyance in his tone. "It would be so much easier if you just spoke to me, you know?"

Melkorka ducked her head for a moment, embarrassed at Hoskuld's words but then rose defiantly, making eye contact as she did so. Pulling his hand away from hers, she marched off.

"I didn't mean it like that," Hoskuld said but didn't follow her.

Not that she cared. Since her pregnancy, her emotions had been all over the place and Melkorka knew that what she felt presently could just as easily be gone a moment later. Right now, though, all she needed to do was to relieve herself.

Following a path leading down to the river, Melkorka pulled off to one side and found a secluded place next to a tree. Using a limb to balance herself, she managed to squat. Her huge belly competed with her as she struggled to maintain her balance. Then, when the task was completed, she endeavoured to pull herself upright once more. Sighing, she wished for her birthing day, for this child to be borne so that she could go back to being able to perform such vital tasks without having to think about every action so carefully.

When finished, she made her way carefully back onto the path and followed it until she reached the river. It was a quiet place, often only inhabited by those who were wishing to make an offering to the gods. Melkorka sat by the river's edge, easing off her shoes and allowing her swollen feet to cool in the frigid waters. Looking upstream, she could see the massive waterfall where people trekked to in order to make their offerings to the gods.

She loved this spot; the view was spectacular and it was relaxing even with the loud crashing of the waterfall. The splash of water over the hard rocks at the bottom calmed her and she closed her eyes so that she could hear it more clearly. Sometimes, she felt like her own gods were speaking to her through the rush of the water and today was no exception.

Melkorka heard footfalls and ignored them. The rush of water gave the sensation that the gods—Eriu's gods—were near. Their presence calmed her, as though protecting her from this strange new land.

And yet, even though this country was unusual, so different from her own, she could feel the pull of it, as though she was always meant to be here. It gave her conflicted emotions as the ache of her homeland had been so quickly replaced with the ache of her love for Laxardal. She could understand entirely why Hoskuld had been so desperate to return to Iceland and show it off to her.

"I am sorry," Hoskuld finally said and Melkorka opened her eyes to look at him.

She was mad and sure that he would realise that just by looking at her. If he wanted to apologise, he could. Let him work hard to get back into her good favour.

He knelt beside her, resting his head against the bulge of her belly. Her fingers itched to run over his braids but she let her hands fall to her sides. The baby inside of her kicked out at the weight of its father and Melkorka smiled, hoping that it had the fiery nature of her own people.

The Icelanders were feisty also but in an entirely different way. Even though they had settled into the farming lifestyle, there was still evidence of their brutality. Melkorka had seen a man stab another outside the great hall merely for being the brother of the man who had killed his father. Their kind were more settled than others in their region but they still attacked and exacted revenge against those who had slighted them.

In a way, Melkorka could now see the nobility of it. The Finngaill made sure that their family was protected and she hoped that her child was fearless like that, to be able to stand up against everything that the world threw at it and not be scared of the repercussions.

However, sometimes she wondered if they spent too much time in revengeful pursuits and not enough building for their future. Her own kind had created a world in which their people could thrive and think beyond those who had slighted them.

This is what she hoped for her child, that he could be fearsome like Hoskuld and his people but also smart enough to see forward and to move beyond the hurt of those around him and strive for better things. Regardless of her standing, she wished there would come a time when her child would know of her heritage and finally meet their grandfather and discover their ways as well.

Hoskuld's hands reached around her expanse and squeezed at her hips. "I never meant to say those words. I am just fearful of losing Olaf. He has been like a father to me over the years and I do not want him to die and leave me behind."

Melkorka finally ignored her firm resolve and looped her fingers through his braided hair. He sighed into the touch and she hoped he didn't think that she could be so easily won over by his words.

Pulling his head up, he gazed at Melkorka. His emotions were plain to see on his face and she softened to him, hating herself all the while.

"I love you, woman," Hoskuld whispered before pulling himself up to kiss her. She turned her head at the last moment, her gaze looking out towards the waterfall and already she felt the urge to urinate once more. "Please don't be mad. I can't stand it when you are like this. It makes my heart want to break."

Melkorka turned back to him, her gaze settling on his and she fought against the hot tears that always seemed to threaten now that she was with child. One hand reached up to swat at her eyes and Hoskuld put his arms around her.

"I am sorry to make you this upset," he said quietly before

tenderly kissing the top of her head. "I deserve your anger but I am still sorry. I hope that you can forgive me."

She felt powerful when he was like this. Hoskuld had purchased her; it should be the other way around. Yet, he allowed her to control him in such a manner. She had seen the same power given by him to Jorunn and Melkorka wondered if it was his personality to give his heart up like this to the women in his life.

With thoughts of Jorunn crossing her mind, she leaned forward and kissed Hoskuld, suddenly overwhelmed with loving him in spite of his wretched faults. He responded immediately and she pushed him down to the ground, instantly hungry for him. It was always this way. She couldn't fight the love she had for him and rather than consider how similar she was to Hoskuld's wife, she swallowed down his affection and allowed herself to be consumed by the moment.

Hoskuld kissed her hungrily and, opening her eyes, she watched the waterfall as Hoskuld loved her in the best way that he could, in the only way that she wanted him to.

ᛗ

THE PAIN WOKE HER.

Sitting upright in bed, she clutched at her belly and groaned into the agony of it. Melkorka bit her lip, trying to stifle the sound even as it escaped. For all of its overwhelming intensity, as soon as the pain had come, it was gone and Melkorka tried to settle back into sleep.

She knew that what she was feeling was birthing pains. Yet, she had heard enough stories of babies being born to know that it would likely be some time yet before she was actively ready to deliver her child. So, she would try and rest for as long as possible.

As she settled into the furs, she rubbed her belly, feeling the tightness of it. Over the last few weeks, her belly has swelled even larger than she thought was possible. Her skin was stretched obscenely as purple marks formed. Now, her stomach was pulled into a peak, the muscles working hard underneath her skin.

Another pain and her stomach clenched once more. She squealed, unable to control the sound. As she relaxed again, she heard movement from across the room.

"Are you alright?" Hoskuld said as he threw open the curtain.

Melkorka nodded even as she could feel another pain gathering. Surely, she wasn't already actively labouring?

As she doubled over, Hoskuld turned. "The baby is coming!"

"She will have plenty of time," Jorunn said, sounding sleepy. "It's only her first."

"I think it is her time already."

"Don't be ridiculous, come back to bed. Let the poor woman be. No need to panic her already."

Hoskuld turned back to Melkorka. "Do you need some help?"

Melkorka nodded. Jorunn might think that her baby was not ready to arrive yet but she had no such confidence. She wanted a midwife, not opinions from a woman who didn't even like her.

"I'm getting Sigrun," Hoskuld said and headed out the door before Jorunn could interrupt once more.

Melkorka felt another pain gathering and pulled the fur up to her face. Biting down on the soft pelt, she hoped to stifle the sound from Jorunn. However, the woman was already in her room. Staring down at her, Melkorka could see the resentment there.

"I hope you die tonight," Jorunn said so softly that Melkorka wasn't even sure that the woman had spoken or if it was merely her own imagination. Another contraction struck then, and she had no more time to think about Jorunn.

By the time Sigrun arrived, Melkorka was writhing in pain

and guttural screams were emanating from her. They came from deep down inside and were filled with the anguish of everything she had been through since her captivity.

More than anything, she wanted her nanny. The woman had always been kind and would be soothing her as she cried through the agony of it all should she be here. In this single moment, she missed her homeland and family more than she ever had before.

"Settle down," Sigrun said, her cool hand laying down on Melkorka's forehead.

Already, she felt more relaxed knowing that the midwife was there. But, more importantly, that Hoskuld had returned and that she was no longer the only adult alone in the house with Jorunn.

"Before long, you will have your sweet child in your arms and this will be a distant memory," Sigrun said. "But, in the meantime, you need to work hard for me."

As Sigrun squatted between her legs, Melkorka felt another contraction building.

"I think it's time to push now," the midwife said before her head popped into view. "You're one of the lucky few that seem to have an easy time of birthing."

Melkorka gathered her strength and bore down, pushing as hard as she could. She pushed until she felt like she was splitting in two and then settled back into the strange sensation of being stretched as the pain subsided once more.

"One more push, whenever you feel the need."

The pain gathered again and Melkorka gritted her teeth and sucked in an enormous breath before expelling it, along with a groan, as she bore down once more. There was the slip of water and blood and then the over-stretched feeling was gone.

On top of that was the squall of a newborn. Before she could speak, to finally do the one thing that she had held back over all this time, a baby was placed into her arms and she looked down upon the perfect form. Even through the blood, she could tell that this child was her everything, that it was the most perfect being ever placed on this earth. She sobbed as she kissed the child's forehead.

"You have a boy," Sigrun said and Melkorka hugged her baby, crying harder.

If she were at home, she would have just produced a son that could draw lineage to one of the most powerful kings in Eriu. This child could still claim that heritage.

However, he also had a different line to lay claim to, a new line of people, and a new country that Melkorka loved in spite of herself. This child was a product of Eriu and Iceland and Melkorka could feel the enormity of it as she hugged the tiny being in her arms.

"A boy," Hoskuld said as he entered the room.

Melkorka looked up through her tears and smiled at the man who was so obviously excited by the news. He came to sit by her. Gazing down at the newborn, he kissed the top of her head. "He is just perfect."

His words mirrored her own thoughts and she had never felt so content. Looking up, Jorunn was at the doorway and Melkorka smiled at her, so happy that she couldn't even be mad at the woman who had hoped for her death earlier in the night. Making eye contact, Jorunn glowered at her before turning and striding from the room.

"I will call him Olaf, in honour of my late uncle," Hoskuld said and Melkorka was proud that he had given the child such a distinction. If she were a slave in her own country and had birthed a child to someone such as Hoskuld, there was no way that the child would be rewarded with a name as important as that of a family member. Her tears flowed harder and Hoskuld pushed back her hair and kissed her sweaty cheek.

The baby squawked once more and Sigrun stepped up to show Melkorka how to help the baby to feed. She smiled once more at Hoskuld as he edged out of the room.

"I will be back in the morning," he said and Melkorka felt

as if nothing could possibly go wrong ever again.

After everyone had left her alone with her newborn babe, Melkorka continued to gaze upon her child.

"I love you, Olaf," she whispered hoarsely.

CHAPTER 20: MELKORKA

"ISN'T IT TIME ALREADY FOR THAT WOMAN TO earn her keep?"

Jorunn was speaking loudly and from her bed, Melkorka could hear the scorn in the woman's voice. As soon as the children had skipped outside, Hoskuld's wife had started. It had been this way every morning for a week now.

Olaf wriggled in her arms. She pushed his hair out of the way as she cooed at him and the child settled down to feed once more. Melkorka was so proud of her son. He was a perfect child in every way, causing her little pain during birthing him, or afterward for that matter. He only fussed when hungry and, already, she could see just how handsome he would grow up to be.

Even through Jorunn's harsh words, she smiled and thanked the gods for her position within the farmstead. While Jorunn wanted her put aside, Melkorka was confident that Hoskuld would not do that.

"She had barely been a mother for a cycle of the moon. There is plenty of time for that later. You know yourself just how hard the first few months are even after you know what to expect."

"I am sick of her sitting around the house as though she is

a queen or some such person. She is our thrall and should be treated as such. Will you really place her above me?"

"Enough, Jorunn," Hoskuld said and Melkorka could sense the discontent there. "I am not putting her before you. Besides, since when have you ever cared about that? I thought that by having this woman here it would allow you your freedom. I cannot understand why you are so jealous of her when you have never been truly interested in me."

The sound of something wooden hitting the table could be heard and Melkorka reached down and kissed Olaf's head. She would not leave. Jorunn was only jealous of the fact that Hoskuld loved her now and not the woman who could never love him in return.

The curtain opened and Hoskuld strode in, feigning a smile as though his disagreement with his wife had never occurred. "How are you this morning?"

Melkorka nodded at him and moved over so that he could sit beside her. He leaned over her and smiled at Olaf.

She couldn't help the way her heart swelled with his action. He loved this child as much as his own to Jorunn and was happy to tell the world about it, even if his wife scowled at him for doing so.

"He is growing strong already and look at how handsome he is," Hoskuld said as he brushed his hand over the baby's head. "Before long, he will be mighty enough to conquer this world."

Melkorka scoffed at him, laughing at his pride. Still, she did believe that her child could do whatever he pleased when he was older. Hoskuld would make sure of that, even in spite of Jorunn.

The curtain flew open once more and Jorunn stormed into the room. Olaf started to fuss and Melkorka kissed his head as she hugged him closer.

"She needs to be gone already!" the woman said, her voice shrill as she raged at her husband. "If she can't work then she needs to be moved on. Sell her off and cut your losses.

Whatever you paid for her, it is too much and now we have nothing to show for it but another mouth to feed!"

So much for Hoskuld's promise that his wife would fall in love with Olaf.

Melkorka covered her son's ears as Jorunn's voice raised even further. She had never seen Jorunn so angry over her before and, for a moment, she wondered if Hoskuld would finally give in to her requests and have Melkorka cast aside. She turned to Hoskuld as he started to speak, trying to make eye contact with him but he was too busy yelling at Jorunn.

"I will not cast aside the woman who has borne a son to me. I would not do it to you and certainly not to her. You can just stop already about this fancy idea that you have in your head. Now that we have so much extra room, there should be no need for this. She stays here with us and you had better get used to it."

The building had been completed not long before Melkorka gave birth. While she still only had her small bedroom, the farmstead had been expanded and Jorunn's children had their own space to call their own.

"Or what?" Jorunn questioned, placing her hands on her hips and raising herself up to stand as tall as she possibly could.

"Enough, Jorunn," Hoskuld said, positioning himself over Melkorka. Olaf was squealing and Melkorka tried to get him to suckle some more. However, she knew that it was the tension in the room that was causing his distress.

"Would you cast me aside for her?"

"Enough, I said. I would not do such a thing. Not even when you are behaving so irrationally. You are my wife and the mother of my children. Your place is here, beside me, no matter how much you don't like it."

Jorunn pursed her lips and stared at Hoskuld. Her face was red and it seemed like she was trying to work out what to say next, holding her breath in the process. Finally, she turned and rushed from the room. A few moments later, the door slammed and Olaf let out an enormous wail in response.

"Shh, sweet child," Hoskuld said and reached over to take the Olaf from Melkorka. Her arms felt bare as he did so, her life empty without her baby in it.

ᛗ

"I WISH THERE WAS another way," Hoskuld said as he lay beside Melkorka.

She stiffened beside him. Olaf was nestled between them, his tiny fingers wrapped around her forefinger. Melkorka wanted to roll over and ignore the entire conversation. Hoskuld had promised her the world. Yet, here she was, in a new world, one that she had somehow fallen in love with, and being cast aside all the same.

Now that Olaf was born, she found that she didn't have the time she had in the past to dwell on her feelings for Hoskuld. It was with clarity in the wee hours of the morning, when feeding Olaf, that she properly delved into their relationship and now saw it without all of the clouding emotions she had before.

Instead of seeing nothing but the affection she felt for Hoskuld or the fact that he treated her so kindly, she now saw how Jorunn controlled him. He may have sought her out because he was feeling unloved. However, he really did have affection for his wife. They shared a common past and had children together. Jorunn was the selection made by Hoskuld and his family. She was the one considered his suitable match regarding familial ties.

Melkorka had heard all of the gossip, of how Jorunn was considered the best catch in the area, and that Hoskuld was the perfect match for her. By comparison, she was merely a side dish, added for flavour to the meal but never intended to replace the meat on the plate.

Looking at Hoskuld, she still felt attracted to the man but

no longer had the time for him that she did before their son was born. Instead, her concerns had shifted to Olaf. Everything she did now was for this child. She would do as she was told in order to protect him and to keep him in good favour with his father and Jorunn. However, she did not have to like it.

Hoskuld was avoiding eye contact with her so she reached out and touched his arm, forcing him to look at her. She implored him, without issuing a single word and he knew her so well that he ducked his head in shame for a moment before replying.

"Olaf will be looked after. You can tend to him as well as us. I will make sure that Jorunn is respectful of that. However, there are plenty of handmaidens here that will help you."

Melkorka nodded her head. It was likely the best scenario for them all. Hoskuld reached over, tucking her hair behind her ear. His fingers lingered at her neck and she tingled under his touch, mad that she still reacted in this way to him. She closed her eyes in an attempt to hide her true feelings but knowing anyway that he would know her inner turmoil.

"I will leave you now but, please, don't think that I no longer have feelings for you. They are just as strong as they were when we were travelling. They always will be."

He kissed her head before standing. Melkorka watched as he left the room and went back to tending their child.

"I will always protect you," she whispered.

ᛗ

"THIS IS A TERRIBLE job, do it again," Jorunn said and Melkorka immediately started unravelling the braids.

She could see no problem with the rows she had just plaited. As she turned to grab the bone comb, Ashildr, the other handmaiden in the room, rolled her eyes and Melkorka smirked in reply.

"I feel like you do not take these tasks seriously," Jorunn continued. "If you do not comply fully, I will have no option but to send you on to someone else. I cannot have thralls that do not know how to attend to me correctly."

Melkorka had unravelled Jorunn's long blonde hair and was brushing it out smooth before braiding it again. Her hair was a glorious pale colour and as smooth as ice on a lake in winter. She wished her own hair was like this. It was so much easier to control and manage than her own red mess of hair that tended to spring out in all directions and tangle in the slightest of breezes. Touching her own tightly formed braids, she was thankful for the Icelandic style that kept it under control.

Her fingers were fast at the task, having had to braid and then rebraid Jorunn's hair every day. Training, Jorunn had called it but Melkorka knew that it was merely punishment. It seemed that Jorunn was never happy and, so far, not a single day had passed when Melkorka hadn't had to braid her hair at least twice.

Olaf started fussing and Melkorka turned, mid-task to cluck at him, hoping that he would settle at the sound.

"Ashildr can tend to him," Jorunn said and the handmaiden immediately headed over to the infant. Melkorka's breasts were heavy, the sound of his noises enough to make her milk come in.

"I think he needs to be fed," Ashildr said, bringing Olaf forward. "Would you like me to continue with your hair?"

"That baby is not hungry," Jorunn replied. "He is merely spoiled. Take him outside Ashildr and let him cry for a while, that will toughen him up to the realities of this world."

Ashildr nodded and Melkorka closed her eyes but the tears were already flowing. She reached out and stroked her son's cheek as Ashildr passed by her.

"I'm sorry," Ashildr mouthed and Melkorka nodded before returning to the task at hand, hoping that this time the work would satisfy the woman and she was then free to go.

As her fingers deftly worked over Jorunn's hair, she could feel the wet of milk spreading. She was uncomfortable and wished to strike out at Jorunn for being so cruel. Yet, her fingers remained steady. She continued to smooth Jorunn's hair and to weave it into tight patterns that were pleasing to the eye.

Melkorka did all of this for Olaf. He was the only person who could control her temper so completely. She did it so that he could thrive in this strange world. If there was a chance that her child could be successful, then she would do anything in her capacity to make it happen. Once again, she thanked the gods for allowing her to birth a son. Even here, they were treasured more completely than girls.

In fact, Olaf would have plenty of opportunities in Iceland. Hoskuld loved him and had given ownership to him in front of his people. Therefore, the child was considered his son and there was no way that could be taken away from him. Melkorka smiled as she worked, thankful to Hoskuld for this small grace.

"Jorunn, what's going on!" Hoskuld's voice was harsh as he entered and it broke into her thoughts, surprising her. She jumped and dropped the hair in her hands. Jorunn's fine hair instantly unravelled and she frowned at the fact that she would have to work longer at completing the task.

"What are you talking about?" Jorunn asked, not at all concerned with Hoskuld's ire.

"Olaf is out there screaming with hunger and you won't allow him to be fed."

Hoskuld banged his hand down on the bench next to Jorunn. As Melkorka brushed out the dropped section of hair, she felt the small bristle of Jorunn's fear and she was glad to have noticed it. The woman was not as confident as Melkorka thought.

"The baby is spoiled and I won't have it. No child is ever better off for being given everything they want as soon as they require it. It is not a good way to bring up this baby and you know it, Hoskuld."

"There is a difference between being spoiled and being hungry. Leave this task, you can feed your child now, woman."

Melkorka did not need to be told twice. She dropped Jorunn's hair once more and darted from the room, following her baby's devastating howls of hunger.

"I am so sorry," Ashildr said as soon as Melkorka came into sight. She snatched her child from the woman and nodded at her. As soon as Olaf latched onto her swollen breast, she smiled at Ashildr to show that she was not mad at her.

Olaf was hiccoughing as he fought to latch on and feed. He was so distraught that bubbles of snot formed and Melkorka wiped them away as soon as they appeared. Standing in the middle of the farmstead, her child fought furiously to drink and she didn't care who saw her.

Finally, Hoskuld appeared. Melkorka now had Olaf perched up over her shoulder as she burped him. She wanted to glare at him but fought against her anger. To finally lose it at him out here, where the other thralls could see would be a mistake. No, she had to bite down on her tongue and rearrange her face into a welcoming smile rather than have anyone suspect that she was angry at Hoskuld for not protecting their child more.

"Jorunn will not do that again," Hoskuld said as he reached her and patted Olaf on the back. "Let's walk."

Melkorka followed obediently, her eyes downturned so that she could not see the curiosity of those surrounding them. Talk would occur now and, while she didn't care for what people said behind her back, she knew that Jorunn would be livid once she heard of it.

When they reached the river, they both sat. His fingers laced through hers and she gazed out over the water rather than concentrate on the warmth in his touch.

"You can now feed Olaf whenever he needs it," Hoskuld said and she nodded at his words. Straightening her back, she was proud that he had gone against his wife's wishes and protected Olaf.

"Jorunn is not happy with my order but she will comply."

Melkorka wanted to ask Hoskuld how he had managed to persuade her to his wishes. He always tried to keep everything fair in his family and it seemed unlikely that Jorunn would simply agree to his instructions. Not when she was so quick to cause distress for Melkorka and certainly not when she knew that Hoskuld could be easily manipulated by her.

Melkorka squeezed Hoskuld's hand and smiled at him when he looked over at her. He kissed her forehead and turned out towards the water, as she had done earlier.

"I am so sorry that your life here has been such a struggle. I honestly didn't think that Jorunn would be so averse to you. Had I suspected it, then I would not have bought you. I never wanted to inflict such pain onto anyone, not you, and certainly not my wife."

Melkorka leaned into his shoulder at his words even though she bristled against them. She needed to make sure that Hoskuld believed in her, in their child, and that she would always love him regardless.

ᛘ

OLAF DASHED ACROSS THE great hall. Melkorka watched him distractedly as she poured wine for Jorunn.

"Careful woman!" Jorunn hissed and Melkorka's gaze darted back to her task. She had not spilled the wine and sighed with relief. Jorunn was only being her usual self and criticising her for nothing at all.

"Mama," Olaf said as he tugged at her skirt.

Melkorka smiled down at her son and reached out to squeeze his cheek. He squealed at her before darting back into the crowd. Other children grouped around him and he was lost in the fray. She was happy to see him so thoroughly accepted by the other youngsters and their families. It was a shame that it was not the same within her own homestead. She bit down on her lip to remind herself not to scowl at Jorunn when she turned back to the woman.

"If I knew better, I swear he just referred to you as his mother," Hoskuld said, leaning over to Melkorka. He patted the space next to him and she sat down, her gaze averted from Jorunn's in case the woman started something up for doing as Hoskuld instructed of her. "Yet, the words he said sounded like nothing I have heard before."

"Stop seeing more in it than what it really is," Jorunn muttered with obvious exasperation. "He is just babbling like a baby does and it means nothing at all."

Melkorka reached out and took Hoskuld's hand. She did it discreetly but knew that Jorunn would see the action. Melkorka may do everything within her power to protect Olaf but she revelled in these small actions that drove Jorunn wild with distraction.

"It is the start of his speech, that is certain," Hoskuld said, trying to appease his wife without backing down on his own belief. "Regardless, he is young to be speaking properly already. Although, I have heard him say distinguishable words and he is not even two years old. He is so clever. I think he will grow to be a fine man."

Melkorka smiled at the praise for her son. However, it was also for the confusion caused by Olaf's word.

He had said Mama, just not in the Icelandic tongue.

Instead, he spoke the language of the Eriu.

CHAPTER 21: JORUNN

THE MARKETPLACE WAS BUSY AS JORUNN made her way through. People jostled against her and she smiled at familiar faces, scowled at thralls that she did not know. Finally, she saw an arm extended in the air and the sound of a familiar voice.

"Over here, Jorunn," Otta called and she smiled broadly at her dear friend.

She wrapped her arms around Otta and hugged her fiercely. The familiar scent of her filled her nostrils and she felt happy for the first time that day.

"It's so good to see you," Jorunn said, her cheek brushing against Otta's as they parted.

"Things are not improving?" her friend asked, taking her hand and leading her away from the rush of people. Leading her down a narrow street, she pulled Jorunn inside her home.

Otta lived on the outskirts of the market, her daily life always filled with bustle. Sometimes Jorunn envied her. The woman had married young, being matched with an old man but one with considerable wealth. She now lived alone, supported entirely because of her dead husband's coin.

Sitting down at the table by the fire, she watched as Otta busied herself with making tea. "Tell me what has happened now."

Jorunn sighed. *Where should she start?*

"That woman is still insolent," she finally said as Otta sat across from her, passing a cup of tea her way.

"Or are you just too expectant of her?" Otta asked and Jorunn wanted to swat at the woman. She knew her far too well.

"I just wish that Hoskuld would do away with her. She is causing even more problems within our marriage than normal. I rue the day that he came home with her."

"Do you think that he did it merely to spite you after your argument?"

Jorunn took a long sip of her tea rather than answer immediately. Jorunn had thought of constantly of that fateful argument and the consequences of it since they had yelled at each other and Hoskuld had left her there, standing on the shoreline, while he had an adventure.

All this time later, she couldn't even remember what had started them off only that it had spiralled down into a mess of past quarrels. Jorunn remembered bringing up every little petty thing that Hoskuld had ever done, her anger scaling up the more she remembered the past.

Eventually, her husband had clenched his fists together. As they stood by the shoreline, him ready to depart and her still goading him on with spiteful words under her breath, she wondered if she had finally gone too far and he was ready to hit her in front of their family and friends. He had caught himself at the last moment, though. His face red with rage but he gritted his teeth and took a deep breath before leaving her behind.

Tuning back into the present day, Jorunn shook her head, trying to free her mind of her past regrets over that argument. She wondered if things would have been different if she had remained calm and allowed him to leave on civil terms rather than flaring up. Would he have returned with only the timber and not a concubine?

"I don't know, Otta."

She fought back a sob, the emotional upheaval of her home life finally catching up. Her friend leaned over, clasping her hand and stilled the tremble in it.

"You can't change the past," Otta said and smiled grimly at Jorunn. "The gods have a purpose for you, and for Hoskuld. All you can do is hope that all will sort itself out sooner rather than later. Perhaps this is the catalyst you both need to move forward in your marriage?"

Jorunn sighed, the sound was harsh and came from deep down inside. They had discussed her loveless marriage countless times over the years. She had even joked that she wished she had married an old man like Otta and now they could both live together and not have to worry about men at all. However, that was not her lot in life and she was still fettered to Hoskuld.

"I feel like I am suddenly pushed to the side. This woman is obviously the shiny new coin that everyone wants for themselves. Hoskuld always defends her, his family and friends also. I just wish that they could look past her beauty and see the spiteful woman behind it all."

Otta squeezed Jorunn's hand once more and she looked up at the woman. Their gaze caught and she wished that she lived here, not with Hoskuld. Life would be so much simpler without having to deal with a husband and his lover.

"I think that maybe you do not see the woman for who she really is. After all, haven't you always wanted Hoskuld to leave you alone?"

Jorunn didn't want this truth thrown at her and she pulled her hand free. Curling it into the other, she laid them both in her lap.

"He is my husband, not hers." It wasn't a good argument, even she knew that. However, it was all that she had. Jorunn was aware that this was the answer to her prayers. Yet, she still felt a jealous rage every time she saw the woman smiling or tending to her baby. "I get enough of this at home, there is no need for you to also back her up."

Jorunn stood suddenly deeply over their conversation.

"I am sorry, I do not mean to upset you, Jorunn," Otta said, also standing. "But I will not lie to you, you know that."

She felt claustrophobic. Not able to look at Otta, Jorunn turned and left her friend behind, ignoring her protests.

The marketplace was bright after the darkness of Otta's home. She squinted against the harsh sun, turning this way and that as her eyes adjusted. Finally, the glare subsided and her surrounds came into stark clarity.

The first person she saw was Hoskuld's woman and she scowled. No matter where Jorunn went, the woman always seemed to be there. Now, not even Otta's place was a safe haven, instead filled with truths that she never wanted spoken of out loud.

"What are you looking at, woman?" Jorunn hissed as she approached. Shoving her shoulder into her, Jorunn pushed against the woman without a name and smiled as she stumbled. "Why don't you go home and tell Hoskuld about how horrible I am? Oh, that's right, you can't. You're nothing but a mute whore, bought because Hoskuld was missing me and wanted to make me madder still than when he left. Don't ever think that you're special, woman. You are nothing more than a purchase made in anger and as a way to make someone else's life a misery."

Jorunn took a deep breath, suddenly feeling better for finally speaking out loud to the thrall about her true purpose. She hoped that the woman would think about her words and question her role within Hoskuld's life. Perhaps it would finally wipe the smug look and adoring gaze from her face.

One final glance towards her as Jorunn left showed the woman's blanched face staring back at her and she laughed heartily as she left.

CHAPTER 22: MELKORKA

"WHO'S A GOOD BOY?" MELKORKA ASKED OF Olaf and the boy squealed at her as he turned and ran away from her outstretched hands.

They were far away from prying eyes and ears. Melkorka was teaching her son the words of her own people and had started speaking in private merely so that she could do so. It was important that Olaf know of her people, of where his heritage lay beyond Iceland.

As soon as Olaf began cooing and making strings of gibberish words, Melkorka had made sure to take some time out from her duties to teach Olaf her language. Now, at the age of two, he was already well on his way to being competent in talking in her language as well as Hoskuld's. So far, he could only string words together but what he said was distinguishable as to what he meant.

Melkorka was worried that he would alert Hoskuld about her ability to speak but the child seemed to know that it was a secret just for the two of them and maintained his own silence on the matter. Well, until he had called her Mama in her own language.

The memory still gave her a strange shiver. She was fearful that Olaf would betray her unintentionally and she would have to explain herself. She wondered if she should speak up first, finally giving Hoskuld what he had wanted for all these years. However, with their relationship presently less than perfect, her silence still felt like control and it was something that she treasured. No, she would remain silent on the matter. It was what she did best after all.

"Olaf, come here baby, let your mama hug you."

Her son turned and rushed towards Melkorka. He leaped at her and she spun him around even though he was getting so big now. As soon as he was in her arms, he was wriggling to be free. Though, once out of her embrace, he ran off, readying himself for another attack.

He loved her more than anything else in this world and it made her feel cherished. Finally, she had found her place and she had never expected it to be because of a son borne into her life as a thrall.

Olaf beamed at her as he hurried forward and she reached out her arms again, ready to catch him. She giggled at him and the flash of Jorunn's smug laugh darted across her vision as she did so.

She had been trying not to think about Jorunn ever since the encounter in the marketplace. Even now, she felt the heat of embarrassment at the woman's words. Jorunn had been right, though.

All along, she had questioned Hoskuld's choice while away from home. He had always told her that he wanted a woman who would love him, unlike his wife. And, judging by Jorunn's behaviour, he was true in that regard. However, she had a sneaking suspicion that Jorunn was also right, that she was merely a purchase made in haste and Hoskuld was too polite to pass her on. She felt like a burden, always not quite fitting anywhere except for when Hoskuld held her in his arms after they made love.

And now, when Olaf needed her.

"Your mama loves you more than anything on this earth, don't you forget that, Olaf," Melkorka insisted, still trying to rid her mind of the doubt put there by Jorunn.

She grabbed Olaf and spun him around. He roared into the air, his tiny fists clasped and pummelling the sky with glee.

"Love Mama," Olaf replied and she felt hot tears prick at her eyes. "Olaf Finngaill."

"Yes," Melkorka agreed. "You are a mighty Finngaill just like your brave father."

She may be mad at Jorunn for her harsh words. Melkorka may also question Hoskuld and his reasoning behind bringing her here but she would never criticise him in front of their son. Boys needed to love their fathers, to look up to them and follow in their footsteps.

Hoskuld had made a mess of her life—and Jorunn's for that matter—but he had good qualities that would bode well should Olaf take them on. Even when it came to relationships, Hoskuld tried to keep the peace rather than pit the two women against each other

"You are also a very special boy of the Eriu," Melkorka continued. "And, don't you ever forget that. Your grandfather is Myrkjartan, King of Aileach. You are of royal blood and, one day, I will make sure that everyone knows that, that you are treated with the respect that our bloodline deserves."

"'Jartan," Olaf said, truncating the name and making Melkorka smile.

"Myrkjartan," she said slowly, accentuating the word. It was strange to think that her son saw this name as unique and the accent something that he struggled with.

"Myr-kjar-tan," Olaf replied, copying the way in which she had broken down her father's name.

"That's it!" Melkorka exclaimed, hugging her boy tightly as she did so and he squirmed within her arms. Already, he was starting to grow up, to see the world growing around him, expanding beyond her. "Never forget just how much I love you my—"

"Woman?" Hoskuld said and Melkorka spun around in terror.

CHAPTER 23: HOSKULD

"YOU CAN TALK?"

Hoskuld felt the world dropping out from underneath his feet. He had suspected it all along but to finally hear the reality of it was unsettling. Effectively, she had lied to him all these years and that crushed him.

Her voice was harsh, croaky, not at all what he expected. At first, when he heard the sound, he thought an old woman had been talking to his son and had paused, listening, trying to work out who it was before he intruded. He knew everyone in Laxardal, so he was surprised at the strange voice.

Then, when the words were not making sense, he realised that the person spoke in another language and so too did his son. That had piqued his interest further.

Over time, his wife had become worse regarding her behaviour towards the thrall. Hoskuld didn't begrudge the time by themselves, he could totally understand it. However, he was curious to know where they went and what they did.

So, this morning, when he saw them depart, he hadn't hesitated to follow them. Keeping his distance, though, he had assumed with the sound of the female voice, that they had met with someone.

He gazed upon the woman, who was looking down at the

ground, not willing to make eye contact with him and demanded an answer. "Explain yourself to me, woman!"

His words came out gruff and he immediately felt terrible. Hoskuld knew that his ire would not get him what he wanted. Yet, he was angry. Over all of this time, she had been lying to him, pretending that she couldn't speak, regardless of whether he believed her or not. And, on some level, he was hurt that she didn't trust him enough to open up to him the way in which she did to their son.

"Please, talk to me," Hoskuld said. His words were softer but he suspected she would still note the undercurrent of venom there.

"Papa," Olaf said, running towards him. Hoskuld scooped the child up as he jumped at him. He swung the boy around and listened to his babyish giggle of excitement as he did so.

"You and your mother have been keeping secrets, I see," he said as he placed the boy back on the ground.

Looking towards the woman, he could see that his words had the required reaction. Hoskuld knew that she would do anything for her son, that her very life was now centred around protecting him.

Since he was born, it had been very obvious to him that the woman was determined to give Olaf the very best life that she could. He had watched closely as she fought against reacting to Jorunn's harsh words so that she could keep their son in good stead. By doing so, she was protecting him, making sure that her child was still in line with Jorunn's children and that they all shared the same prestige. Hoskuld had known this and he suspected that Jorunn did too, especially considering her ongoing behaviour towards the woman.

"Do not criticise Olaf," the woman said, her voice cracking as she did so.

Her gaze remained downturned and Hoskuld stepped forward. Carefully, he reached out and grasped at her chin, forcing her to look at him. Her eyes were filled with tears and she bit her lip, as though that would somehow hold them back.

"Our son is safe in his position," Hoskuld promised. "Tell me your name."

She blinked and fat tears spilled over. They rolled down her face as she swallowed hard before she finally spoke. "Melkorka."

Hoskuld gasped. Not because her name meant anything to him, or reminded him of someone else but, merely, because he finally knew what to call her. He ran the name through his mind over and over, learning it, getting accustomed to it.

"Who is your family?" he then asked. "Is there truth in what Gilli spoke about all those years ago?"

Melkorka nodded at him but it wasn't enough. He waited for the words to spill along with the tears.

"Mama's crying," Olaf said and Hoskuld turned away from their gaze, effectively breaking it and Melkorka let out a small sob.

"It's alright, Olaf," she finally said, reaching out and hugging the small boy. "Mama's going to speak for Papa for a while. How about you find the flowers for me that I like the most?"

"Sure, Mama," Olaf said but he gave Hoskuld a look that broke his heart.

His own son was unsettled because he had made his mother cry. Hoskuld knew that he had trust to gain back later on and vowed that he would. But, for now, he had more pressing matters.

"I will not harm your mama," he said and smiled. "I would never do that."

"It's true, Olaf," Melkorka said and Hoskuld noted that her voice was starting to even out now. As she continued to speak, it was settling into the way that it should sound.

Olaf nodded at Melkorka before giving Hoskuld one final look and rushing off to pick flowers. He moved towards the meadow but, as Hoskuld watched, he noted that his son remained well within distance to hear what they were saying. Olaf continued to glance their way, even as he searched the field for flowers.

Hoskuld reached out and clasped the woman's—no, Melkorka's—hand. She allowed it but didn't squeeze his hand in return. He led her to a place to sit and then sat down beside her. "Tell me everything."

Melkorka sighed before looking out over the meadow. She smiled at Olaf when he waved at her and returned the action.

"My father is the Eriu king called Myrkjartan. We lived near the Grianan of Aileach."

"What is that?" Hoskuld asked.

He wasn't entirely sure that he believed everything she was saying. However, over the years he, along with others, had questioned her lineage. She had always held herself as the entitled did and had never truly presented as a commoner. So, while he pulled himself away from the situation and tried to look at it through impartial eyes, Hoskuld also believed that what she was saying was true.

"It is a fort, built to protect my people from the Finngaill, from the likes of your kind."

She looked up as she revealed this information. Her gaze was harsh, as though by speaking the words she was remembering and returning to the time before he had owned her, to when he truly was the faceless enemy.

He had hoped that over the years she would grow to love him. In fact, he thought she did. She was always respectful towards him, always glad to see him, compliant between the furs, willing and even suggesting towards it. Even now, with their strained relationship, there were still moments of what he thought were true affection. He had never had reason to believe that she didn't love him.

Until now.

Was it all just an act?

His heart sank. Had he walked from a relationship such as he had with Jorunn, an honest relationship, yet a loveless one, into one that appeared filled with love on the surface but was merely further deceptions underneath? He hoped not. Because this sort of relationship felt worse than the one that he had with Jorunn if he was being entirely truthful with himself.

He could also feel the small snaking fear rising at the fact that Melkorka had never truly trusted him. If she had, she would have opened up to him. She would have spoken well before now. He had asked her so often in the past, requesting her to vocalise her opinion and yet she had refrained.

"How were you taken?" Hoskuld merely asked the question in order to distract himself from his own dark thoughts.

"I am not sure who it was," Melkorka said.

She was picking at a loose thread on her skirt and Hoskuld reached out to take her hand. Melkorka stopped her relentless task but her fingers twitched under his touch, as though they really wanted to continue. Hoskuld held on tightly, regardless.

"They were merely there one day," she continued. "I was out in the woods when they came and I tried to get back to the fort. I never made it, though."

"I am sorry that you went through that," Hoskuld said quietly. "Our kind can be terrible in that regard. Although to be fair, my people, here in Iceland, are no longer great raiders. We prefer to stay put and build up our own population. This land is bountiful and special. We no longer feel the need to go looking for better prospects."

"Yet, you still purchase the spoils," Melkorka said.

"Yet, we do. I am sorry for that. However, would you prefer that someone, like the ones who took you originally, purchase you? How would you like living from raid to raid with those brutes?"

Melkorka was silent, her gaze following Olaf as he dashed across the meadow, chasing a critter in the long grass. He squealed as he did so.

"Perhaps it would have been better if they had killed me,"

she finally said and Hoskuld felt the honest truth of it.

Leaning in, he rested his head against hers. His arm wrapped around her shoulders and he pulled her closer as he tried to swallow down the resentment starting to establish itself. Her lack of speech now felt like an ongoing betrayal.

He pushed aside those thoughts and tried to concentrate on learning more about Melkorka, about finding out the truth of her. Hoskuld was worried that if he showed anger towards her now, she would close up once more and he would never discover another thing about her.

"Maybe you are right. However, it would never have given me the chance to meet you, or for Olaf to have been born. Sometimes life is hard for a reason. The gods only truly test those who are worthy."

"I believe the gods, whether they be yours or mine, had a purpose in bringing us together. However, it doesn't stop my desire to be a part of my homeland. It doesn't stop me from desperately missing my family. The ache has not ceased over the years, no matter how much I have fallen in love with this new country."

Hoskuld was surprised by the admission. He was glad that she felt at home here, even if she missed her own country.

"We must tell Jorunn of this," Hoskuld finally said.

Melkorka froze in his arms but he was determined to reveal the truth to his wife. After all of these years, she needed to know how badly she had been treating the daughter of a king.

"IT'S THE TRUTH," HOSKULD said, trying to reason with Jorunn.

"Are you joking?" she retaliated. "Or are you simply a fool?"

Internally, Hoskuld shied away from the words. On the

outside, though, he stood tall, not letting his wife know that she wounded him.

"You've heard the rumours over the years," Hoskuld reasoned. "We have all suspected it."

"A few words spoken by a supposed mute does not make them the truth, though. If she has lied about being able to talk for all of these years, then what's stopping her from lying about everything?"

"You can't deny it," Hoskuld continued. "You know it is the truth."

"I most certainly do not!" Jorunn screeched at him. She threw her hands in the air for emphasis. "You are a bigger fool than even I suspected. I don't care what you or she says and I will not treat the woman any differently because of it. You can believe her lies and fanciful imaginings but I won't. You know she is merely trying to come between us. That is all that she has ever wanted."

Hoskuld stopped short with the words. "Is that what you truly believe?"

"It's what I know."

"I have never wanted you to feel that way," Hoskuld said quietly. "I always thought that you never wanted me, that by getting another woman, you would be free to have your own life, to do as you pleased. I never thought that you really wanted me."

Jorunn sat down suddenly, as though the wind had pushed her over, except there was no breeze within their home. Stepping forward, Hoskuld came to settle down next to her. He wanted to reach out and touch Jorunn's hand but it had been so long that he didn't know how to. With Melkorka it was easy. With his wife, it was as if he had to stretch across a great chasm that was as deep as it was wide.

"I have never wanted you in the way you needed," Jorunn finally said. The words were forced, as though she didn't really want to own up to her true feelings and Hoskuld wondered why they had not had this conversation earlier in their marriage. "I still needed you, though."

Hoskuld was shocked that Jorunn had finally admitted her true weakness. He reached out and took her hand. Jorunn squeezed tightly as soon as they touched.

CHAPTER 24: MELKORKA

MELKORKA MADE HER WAY SLOWLY BACK TO the homestead. She was unsure of herself and her gait reflected her indecision. Olaf, on the other hand, dashed forward. He stopped only to hurry her along.

"Mama! Come on, I'm hungry."

She smiled at her son and continued her slow meander. It was cold, the wind was whipping up as dusk blew in with it. Still, she dragged her feet.

Even with her hesitation, the house she shared with Hoskuld eventually came into sight. Olaf bustled through the door, announcing his presence and she could hear Hoskuld chuckling at him.

She sighed, pausing as she did so. Looking skyward, she wished for the stars to be out already. They comforted her. Just the knowledge that these same stars also looked down upon her family in Eriu was enough to keep her going. But only if she could see them.

"Where's your mother?" Hoskuld said.

Her son replied in his usual manner, dashing through his words. Some came out clear, others still new to him.

Olaf was always busy, always eager to rush forward into the world. She was jealous of him. The luxury of being born a boy was something that she would never know. Standing on the outside looking in, she already knew that his life would be much easier than hers.

What would Jorunn think of her now? Melkorka thought.

She was certain that Hoskuld would have revealed everything to his wife already. The only question that remained was whether or not the woman would finally believe him.

Melkorka knew the answer as soon as she braved stepping through the door.

"Oh, look, her royal highness is here," Jorunn said and Melkorka scowled at the woman before ducking her head. "Let me dust off this chair for you, Queen of the Liars."

Melkorka swallowed hard as she moved through the house. The aroma of stew greeted her but her stomach clenched up tightly and the scent of the fat in the meat made her feel like being sick.

"What, are you not going to speak?" Jorunn continued. "Surely you have plenty to say to me, finally, after all of this time. I bet you have been saving it all up. Let me have it, I can certainly stand up against your spite."

Melkorka raised her gaze once more. She shot Jorunn another venomous look before stalking off to her bed.

"Leave the poor woman alone," Hoskuld said but his words came too late for Melkorka to take comfort in them.

The darkness of the room enveloped her and she was thankful for the oblivion of it. Laying down, she waited for sleep to overtake her jangled emotions. Exhausted with the effort of the afternoon, of the shock of finally being found out, Melkorka prayed to her gods to help her to sleep, to forget about everything.

However, the gods did not comply.

Instead, she ran the events of the day over and over in her head until the glow of a candle warmed her eyelids. Melkorka opened her eyes to it before she realised that Jorunn in the room.

She had hoped that it was Hoskuld, ready to side with her, as he always had in the past. However, this time, he was remarkably absent. Melkorka felt more alone in this moment than she ever had before, even when she was dumped into the care of Gilli, even as she was being grabbed by the brute who would change her life forever.

"I am ready for bed," Jorunn said.

Hoskuld's wife stood in the middle of the room and Melkorka was tempted to ignore the woman. She was tired and the last thing she wanted to do was attend to someone filled with such malice towards herself.

Instead, she raised herself from her bed and dusted down her clothing, smoothing the material before following Jorunn back to her own quarters.

"Ouch, you are pulling my hair," Jorunn said as Melkorka untied her apron but she knew that the woman was lying. Melkorka was nowhere near Jorunn's hair which was tucked up into a braided bun at the nape of her neck. "Speak, woman, now that I know that you can. You need to apologise for your behaviour."

Melkorka sighed softly, trying to swallow it back even as it came out of her mouth. So, that was what Jorunn wanted, to get her to speak to her. Well, even though she could, even though she had been found out today, she would not give Jorunn the satisfaction of hearing her voice. It was a special secret, one she reserved for her son and, now, Hoskuld. She would remain silent to those who still antagonised her.

Melkorka concentrated on her task. Undoing the leather thongs holding together Jorunn's robe. She made sure that she was gentle, that she went nowhere near the woman's hair, that she maintained a distance that wasn't considered to be too close, too personal. Still, Jorunn found fault within her work.

"You're pulling the laces too tight!"

She wasn't. Melkorka was pulling the robe outwards, ready to lift the item of clothing up and over her head once the woman had stopped complaining and lifted her arms in compliance.

Jorunn's voice was loud, shrill, and she knew that it was for the benefit of everyone else in the house. It had been some time since she had tried to curb her behaviour towards Melkorka in front of her children. Even Olaf ignored the open hostility, since he was that accustomed to it.

Melkorka ignored the woman's rantings and started lifting the robe up over Jorunn's midsection. She stepped in closer as she did so, unable to maintain the previous distance while she attempted to interact with the woman.

"What are you doing?" Jorunn fumed, turning as she did so. "Get out of my face!"

Melkorka stepped back, dropping Jorunn's clothing and crossed her arms. Glaring at the woman, she was tempted to storm from the room.

Let the horrid woman do her own tending. See how far she got with it.

She waited patiently, or so it seemed on the surface as her face settled into a bland expression now that she had finished glaring at the woman. Her crossed arms were the only indication that she was angry.

Jorunn looked her up and down and Melkorka refused to flinch under the scrutiny. Instead, she squared her shoulders and lengthened her spine. She would no longer falter under this woman. Jorunn did not scare her. Inside, a rage was swirling. Fueled by years of living under the instruction of this woman, the wife of her lover, she was ready to explode.

"You lazy woman!" Jorunn said, still provoking her.

Melkorka maintained her gaze as Jorunn started pulling off her own stockings. The woman's lips were pursed so tightly together that Melkorka couldn't even see the normal rosy colour of them.

Then, Jorunn spoke softly, this time a personal note rather than for the benefit of the household. "I knew that Hoskuld picked you to spite me, that your beauty was the only thing that attracted him, knowing that it would anger me further."

Melkorka frowned at the words. Hoskuld and his wife had quarrelled prior to his purchase of her but he had explained it differently, that he was after companionship after years of a loveless marriage. While Melkorka thought that Jorunn was merely speaking her own mind or making things up to hurt her, the words stuck in her mind. It only added fuel to what Jorunn had said to her in the marketplace and now she wondered how much of her life was based on lies between the married couple.

"Get over here and help me," Jorunn seethed, her voice now loud again. Melkorka stepped forward, the years of conditioning an instant reaction even though she didn't want to do it.

Then, her mind caught up with the action of her body and she halted once more. Rather than tend to the woman, Melkorka shook her head, her defiance evident to Jorunn and the woman's eyes narrowed to evil slits against her.

Perhaps she had gone too far. The image of Olaf flashed through her mind and she was scared for a moment. Everything she did now would impact on her son's life. However, the rage swirled up, covering her vision with a red haze and she actually snarled at the woman.

Stepping forward, Jorunn flicked out her stockings and released them at Melkorka. Like a whip, they struck her. Her face stung where they made contact and the deed finally released the rage inside.

After all of these years, after being controlled by everyone around her, Melkorka finally snapped.

Her silence had been enough to control the rage. She had used it as a weapon against those who held her captive. But, more importantly, the knowledge that she had kept something so important hidden for all of this time had been enough.

Now that Hoskuld had discovered her secret, her anger was like a beast being released on everyone around her.

Reaching out, Melkorka wrapped her fingers around the stockings as they lost momentum and before Jorunn could pull them back for another attempt. Yanking them towards her, she laughed openly at the look of surprise on Jorunn's face.

Pulling hard on the stockings, Jorunn rushed forward, unable to stop herself before they crashed together. Melkorka stood tall, her body unmovable against the slight woman. Without even considering the consequences, Melkorka pulled back her arm as her fingers curled into a fist.

Releasing all of her fury, Melkorka smashed it into Jorunn's face. She felt the crack of gristle in Jorunn's nose and a warm spurt of blood sprayed across her face. Smiling, Melkorka stepped back, allowing the woman to stagger and drop.

Jorunn wasn't done, though. Ignoring the blood dripping into her mouth, she then threw herself against Melkorka.

It was her turn to be surprised by the attack. Staggering, Melkorka had to take a couple of steps before she gathered her weight back underneath herself.

A primal scream was building and, as it unfurled, Melkorka threw herself at the woman. They crashed together once more. This time each reached for the other and they fell to the floor. Rolling around, Melkorka pulled back her fist and tried to make contact again. Jorunn knew what to expect, though, and rolled away, taking Melkorka with her. Letting go, Jorunn tried to slap her in return.

All the time, Melkorka's scream filled the room.

"I will kill you!" Jorunn roared in reply and Melkorka dug her nails into the woman. If she couldn't hit her, the least she could do was use other means to inflict more pain.

"What's going on!" Hoskuld's voice shattered their violent embrace. Pausing for a moment, Jorunn looked up at her husband and Melkorka finally got her moment to punch the woman again. The clack of her jaw as her teeth clattered together gave Melkorka an immense satisfaction, as did the further splay of blood from the woman's broken nose.

Stepping in, Hoskuld yanked at the back of her clothing, pulling her free from his wife. Melkorka fought against him as he dragged her back across the room. Her arms flailed out in an attempt to slap Jorunn once more but Hoskuld was too strong, too quick, and she was unceremoniously dumped into a corner.

Leaping forward, Jorunn gathered for another attack and Hoskuld put out a hand to stop her. "Enough!" he roared at them both.

But it wasn't nearly enough for Melkorka. She has spent so long with a simmering rage inside that her whole body trembled in response. The anger burned inside, rippling along her spine like a wave in a storm and she arched back against the wall behind her.

Pushing herself forward, she ran at Jorunn. They clashed again, their fingers reaching out, tangling in each other's hair. Jorunn's locks may have been pulled back into a bun to begin with but Melkorka's deft fingers twisted into it and pulled great clumps free.

"Mama?" Olaf's frightened little voice was what finally broke through to Melkorka.

The rage ebbed away with the sorrow in her son's single word and she had no choice but to slump to the floor, defeated.

Olaf was rushing at her, getting between Melkorka and Jorunn and jumping into her lap.

Realising the enormity of the situation, Melkorka hugged at her son and hoped that she would be able to see him again after this night was over.

"It's alright, Olaf," she whispered into his ear as her tears mingled in his hair.

CHAPTER 25: HOSKULD

HOSKULD GAZED OUT ACROSS THE landscape. The scenery was beautiful and it conflicted greatly with what he was feeling on the inside.

His life was a mess.

He was genuinely regretting his choice made to purchase Melkorka. Usually, any remorse he had was tempered with the knowledge that the gods had willed the events in his life and he had no say in the matter. He also always looked to his son, Olaf, for reassurance that he had done the right thing. Now, for the first time, he couldn't even use Olaf to help calm his emotions.

Instead, he thought of Melkorka, of his wife, Jorunn, of the mess of his life and he honestly didn't know what to do. After all of his time married to Jorunn, he had never felt such conflicting thoughts regarding their relationship.

When Melkorka arrived, he merely thought her jealousy was making her react the way that she did. Surely, she didn't have feelings for him beyond that. Now, he didn't know. With all of her jealousy towards Melkorka shining through, Hoskuld swore that Jorunn was acting as though she did want him, that she always had but hadn't had the knowledge of how to truly show it.

As for Melkorka, well, he shook his head at the thought. She was the mother of his child, his new shining boy that had so much potential. And, she had shown Hoskuld affection almost from the start, the very thing which he was craving so much that he had bought a thrall rather than approach his wife.

Now, he had no idea of what to think of their relationship. She had struck out at Jorunn. There had been a fight and, regardless of who started it, he had to side with his wife against her because that was what Jorunn was insisting.

She had desperately begged him to send Melkorka away. He could see the grief in her face as she cried out her fears. Jorunn had begged for them to start afresh, to finally be the husband and wife that they should have been from the start and Hoskuld ached for the possibility.

For all that Melkorka had given him, he had only ever wanted a decent marriage. Jorunn had been a fine selection at the time and he hoped they would grow into their marriage such as his own parents, who hadn't had love at the start. However, their relationship had grown over the years because that was what they both wanted.

Jorunn had been different. She had always looked outside of their marriage for... something. Hoskuld wasn't even sure that she knew what it was that she wanted. Yet, he had stayed by her side, watching her yearn for the impossible thing that even she couldn't define.

Until Melkorka had arrived.

Then, his wife channelled everything into her rage against the younger, prettier woman. She had been determined to make all of their lives miserable from that time onwards. Melkorka had managed, somehow, to travel through the dangers of their household and maintain some sort of credibility.

"Hoskuld?" Jorunn's voice startled him out of his thoughts and he waited for her to sit down next to him.

She gazed out over the landscape, as he had been doing.

Jorunn was calm now, her face still puffy with tears and a long red scratch ran down one cheek. But it was the black smudges under her eyes and her swollen nose that was the utter giveaway that a battle had been waged. Hoskuld reached up and gently touched her face. She didn't flinch, only closed her eyes and Hoskuld felt ill with all of the conflict that he had caused this woman. The mother of his children deserved better.

Both of them did.

"What are we going to do about this mess?" he asked and Jorunn sighed as she opened her eyes and looked towards him.

"She needs to go," she replied quietly.

It was Hoskuld's turn to close his eyes and he swallowed hard against the notion that Jorunn was absolutely right in the matter. He nodded his reply and Jorunn leaned in to rest her head on his shoulder.

HE FELT MELKORKA'S GAZE on him as soon as he entered his home, even though he could not see her. Holding hands with Jorunn, he wanted to pull away, to not hurt Melkorka's feelings more but that would further inflict pain on his wife.

Always, an impossible choice.

"I need to talk to Melkorka," he said as they released their hold.

She nodded at him before heading towards the fireplace.

Melkorka was not in sight but he knew that he would find her in her bedroom. As he approached, her eyes came into focus out of the gloom and his heart broke with the agony he saw there.

"Please, come for a walk with me," Hoskuld said, holding out his hand to her.

The woman blinked at him, slowly, as though deliberating her answer.

Eventually, she stepped out of the dark and towards the light. Melkorka did not take his offered hand, though. Instead, with chin held high, she marched out of the room and strode across the open area. Not even looking towards Jorunn, she opened the door and left the building.

Glancing at his wife, Hoskuld could see the stiff way in which she held her shoulders as she tried to concentrate on preparing the evening meal.

Exiting the house, he scanned the landscape for Melkorka. Already, she was far ahead, on her way to the river, the one place that seemed to bring her true comfort in Laxardal. He hurried to catch up. Stepping alongside, he wanted to reach out, to hold her hand but hesitated.

Melkorka did not look at him as he caught up to her and he did not want to provoke more rage from the women in his life. That would come later when he had a chance to tell Melkorka of his plans. It was the only option but he knew that she would not be happy with the arrangement. Still, he hoped to salvage some sort of relationship with her, for the sake of their child, at least.

"Can we stop here?" Hoskuld finally asked.

As the sun dropped lower in the sky, the harsh glare of it danced across the water, creating a glittering wonderland. The beauty of it was lost on Hoskuld as he sat down.

Melkorka stood, obviously not prepared to be in close proximity to him and the action wounded him.

"I am sorry for the struggles you have had daily, living here with Jorunn and me," Hoskuld started. Melkorka couldn't even look at him. Instead, she scanned the horizon and waited for him to continue. "I really thought we could have a good life together, that Jorunn would be fine with the arrangement. I regret that it has not worked out that way."

"You are speaking as if it is all coming to an end," Melkorka said.

There was a wicked edge to her tone and Hoskuld sunk further into his seated position. She was not going to make this easy for him. Nor should she.

"I can't have you treat Jorunn in the manner that you did. She is my wife and, regardless of how the disagreement started, I have to think of her wellbeing above yours, even though that hurts me."

He was desperately trying to soften the blow before it arrived but Melkorka's arms crossed over her body and her fingers dug in tightly before she turned to face him.

"What is to become of me?"

At least she didn't try to beg for his forgiveness or to make him see that it was entirely Jorunn's fault. She could outside of all the clutter. As much as it hurt him, he was thankful for her stoic approach for her lack of emotion in the present situation.

Looking at the harsh set of her jaw, it was as if everything she felt for him had drained out with the bitter argument with Jorunn earlier. He was sad to see only the shell of the woman he had fallen for over the years. It was a loss, almost like a death to know that their relationship had been ruined so completely in the span of a single day.

Although maybe it had always been a precarious situation, only Hoskuld had never seen it. With all of Melkorka's silence, he could only guess at her true emotions over the years.

Had he imagined more into their relationship than was ever warranted? His heart dropped with the realisation that he might have loved her more than she had ever done so in return.

"I do not want to see you cast away," Hoskuld finally said. "However, I cannot stand for your behaviour earlier. Even still, I want you to continue to be a part of my life."

He chanced a glance towards her and he noted that Melkorka's eyes darted away. Her lips pursed and he reached forward, finally giving in to the need to touch her, to measure her reaction to him. It had always been the only way in which he could ever gauge her feelings for him, after all. She flinched but he managed to clasp two of her fingers and held on tightly.

"I will set you and Olaf up with your very own house," Hoskuld started. The fact that he finally had a use for all the leftover timber was not lost on him either. "It will give you standing within the community, as I know that is important to you. Olaf will be considered—always—as my child and I will endeavor to make sure that everyone in Laxardal is aware of this. However, you can no longer stay under the same roof as Jorunn."

"Was I ever more than revenge towards Jorunn?" Melkorka asked.

Hoskuld closed his eyes, unable to look at her.

"I loved you, even at the start, I think," he said, avoiding the question. "I still do. It is complicated, however."

"How can it be complicated? Either you purchased me in order to prove something to your wife or you didn't."

Hoskuld clenched his jaw. He wanted to be anywhere but here. Already, he had had a tangled mess of a relationship with his wife and he did not want to repeat it all again with Melkorka.

"Perhaps the gods gave me a reason to make an impossible choice in order to give me the happiness that I so desired," he said, mirroring the words he had said to her once before.

Melkorka nodded before pulling her fingers from his grasp.

CHAPTER 26: MELKORKA

THE BUILDING WAS STARTING TO TAKE SHAPE and Melkorka hugged Olaf as the men worked hard to get the house finished.

Gazing upon the hewn planks, she remembered back to when she had watched Hoskuld chopping them down. Melkorka had been so hopeful then. She was now, too, but it was a different kind of hope. Whereas she had been dependent on Hoskuld to bring her happiness, now she only relied on herself and that made her heart swell more than she could have ever imagined.

It has been hard of late. Melkorka had stayed in the background, not wanting to see Jorunn and provoke her ire further.

However, hiding from Hoskuld had been harder.

He still thought that their relationship had the potential to flourish. However, Melkorka knew the truth of the matter. They were doomed and always had been. Ever since she had been sold to him and she chose to remain silent, the opportunity for failure was what their love had been based on.

From the very start, there had been nothing but deceit, on both sides. She had aimed to be in charge of her situation with her silence and he had controlled her on a more basic level, by way of a transaction of silver.

There had been love there, of that Melkorka had no doubt. However, they were merely instruments to the gods and their time together was no longer viable.

Melkorka squinted against the heat of the sun, her hand raised up to cover her eyes and saw the landscape stretching out in front of her. Olaf struggled to pull free and was now racing across the open plain, in pursuit of some small critter.

"He is a fine lad," Hoskuld said, coming to stand next to her.

"Of course, he is," she replied.

She didn't need reassurance that he was perfect. Melkorka had raised him, had tended to his every need over the past two and a half years and knew this to be true already.

"It is all thanks to you, Melkorka."

It was strange to hear her name being spoken by one of the Finngaill. It sounded unusual even though it rolled off his tongue in such a delightful manner. She nodded her response, unsure of how to answer him.

"Papa!" Olaf called as soon as he saw his father and raced back across the field.

"Olaf!" Hoskuld returned and swung the boy up into the air. "You are getting so big and strong. You will be ready for the king's army before long."

"I like it here," Olaf said as soon as Hoskuld swung him back down to the ground.

"I am glad. You are big enough to be the man of the house now and I thought it might be best if you took your place there sooner rather than later my brave boy."

Melkorka rolled her eyes at Hoskuld's response, wanting to speak out and set his words straight. She didn't like her son to know of lies, to believe words merely because they had been spoken. However, she kept her mouth closed. There was plenty of time to explain all of this to him later.

After all, she now had her own home, her own family, her own place in this world and no one else could take it away from her.

Well, that was almost true. There was one thing left that bound her.

"I want to be set free from your ownership," she said when Olaf darted off to help one of the men carrying a long length of wood. "It is the first and last thing I will ever ask of you."

Turning, she watched Hoskuld's face. His jaw clenched as his gaze flickered across the landscape. Eventually, his gaze lowered, settling on her and she felt the familiar flicker of desire that she always felt for this man. Even against everything that had happened, she still hoped for something more. Gritting her teeth, she swallowed back her fanciful notions and stared back towards her son.

There was no time for love in this relationship anymore. After all of these years, Melkorka had learned one thing about Hoskuld and that was that he loved his family.

And, Olaf was his family, not her.

Melkorka would always fall to the wayside when it came to Jorunn, no matter how much he denied it. She had to understand that first and foremost so that she could move forward in her life.

"I grant you that right," Hoskuld said and Melkorka

sobbed involuntarily. "You are a free woman from this time forth."

The words surprised her and she looked at Hoskuld, expecting she had imagined them. He looked down at her grimly and her heart broke for him. In all of this mess, he had only hoped for happiness. She wished that he would find it with his wife, even if it meant that Melkorka lost out in the end.

But, she hadn't really.

Turning, Melkorka's gaze followed the lay of the land. She peered over the open meadow and further outwards until her sight finally rested on the massive volcano that dominated the landscape.

Melkorka was free

The excitement of the situation swelled inside of her, filling her heart in a different way to her previous love for Hoskuld. With the weight of her captivity so suddenly gone and a horizon of endless possibility now presenting itself, Melkorka even dared to wonder if she would ever see her homeland again, if her father would learn of her fate.

Olaf darted across her line of vision and she smiled. One day, when he was a man, she hoped that he would travel to Eriu. She had taught him the language after all.

His kind always travelled, always sought out the world. Perhaps he would travel for her—or even take her with him—as he sought out his other family.

Melkorka had fought hard to maintain Olaf's place within this world. However, there was an easier way in which she could guarantee his position. If she could prove for certain that he was the grandson of a king than his place would be guaranteed.

By way of her heritage, he would rank higher than Jorunn's children. Even though she was a woman, her son would retain her lineage—only if she could prove it.

As she touched her golden armband, the one that had been a birthing gift from her parents, she smiled. If it was the last thing she would do, it would be to wipe any doubt from Jorunn's mind that she was better than Melkorka and her son.

If you enjoyed this book, please make sure to leave a review on Amazon and Goodreads. A long review is not needed, just adding a short sentence or two helps other potential readers find this book.

You can also join my mailing list in order to find out when the second book in Melkorka's saga, *The Peacock's Mother*, is ready to purchase.

A MAP OF MELKORKA'S WORLD

The world that Melkorka and Hoskuld lived in can been seen in the map below, using the common names for each area in the Viking Age as well as the places we now know them. Names in all capital letters, (i.e. SWEDEN) are the current titles. However, during the Viking Age, these areas were less defined or only known by the other name places indicated (i.e. Gotaland).

This map was originally developed from a public domain satellite image that was kindly provided by Koyos (commons.wikimedia.org/wiki/File:Norden_satellite.jpg).

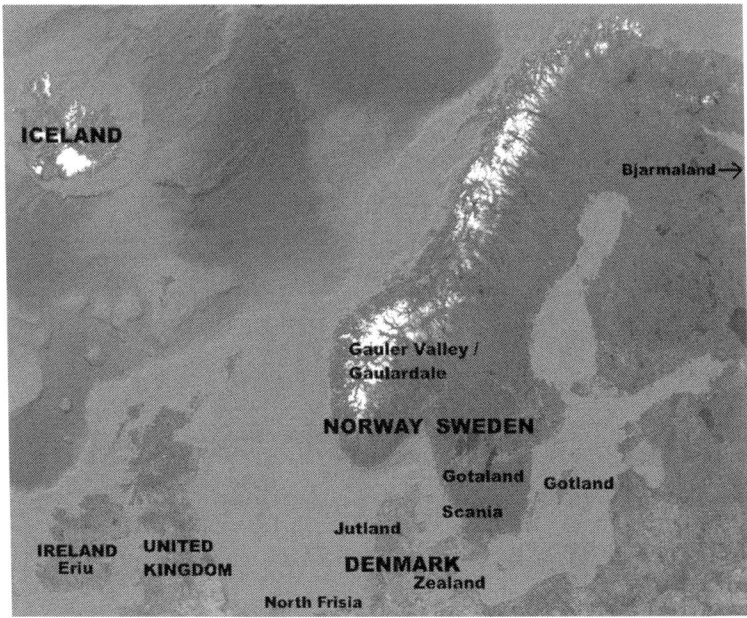

Some of the common alternative names for these areas can also be found below:

Gaular: Gaulardale, Gaular Valley, Fosselandet (the land of the waterfalls).

Götaland: Gotaland, Gautland, Gothia, Gothenland, Gothland.

Gotland: Gottland.

Skania: Skane, Skåne.

Jutland: Jütland, Cimbric or Cimbrian Peninsula, Den Kimbriske Halvø, Kimbrische Halbinsel, Cimbricus Chersonesus, Denmark.

Zealand: Sjælland, Denmark. It should be noted that Zealand should not be confused with Zeeland, which is located in Holland.

MELKORKA'S TALE: AS TOLD IN CHAPTERS TWELVE AND THIRTEEN OF THE *LAXDÆLA SAGA*

Fans who have read my previous books in the *Vikings Secrets* series, will know that I like to include the original saga following my fictional retelling. Melkorka's tale is no exception and her portion of the saga featured in *The Irish Viking Princess* this story is included below.

The passage below of the Laxdæla Saga was originally translated by Muriel A.C. Press (Release Date: February 20, 2006 [EBook #17803] and last updated on June 20, 2012) from an anonymous source and is considered to be in the public domain in the United States. The full version of this translation can be viewed in its entirety via the Project Gutenberg (gutenberg.org), an online resource dedicated to providing public domain works to all who want to peruse them.

All formatting, grammar, and spelling have been included from the original translation and have not been altered in anyway other than to format into the style used throughout this book.

Chapter XII
Hoskuld Buys a Slave Woman

There were tidings at the beginning of the summer that the king went with his fleet eastward to a tryst in Brenn-isles, to settle peace for his land, even as the law laid down should be done every third summer. This meeting was held between rulers with a view to settling such matters as kings had to adjudge—matters of international policy between Norway, Sweden, and Denmark. It was deemed a pleasure trip to go to this meeting, for thither came men from well-nigh all such lands as we know of. Hoskuld ran out his ship, being desirous also to go to the meeting; moreover, he had not been to see the king all the winter through. There was also a fair to be made for. At the meeting there were great crowds of people, and much amusement to be got—drinking, and games, and all sorts of entertainment. Nought, however, of great interest happened there. Hoskuld met many of his kinsfolk there who were come from Denmark. Now, one day as Hoskuld went out to disport himself with some other men, he saw a stately tent far away from the other booths. Hoskuld went thither, and into the tent, and there sat a man before him in costly raiment, and a Russian hat on his head. Hoskuld asked him his name.

He said he was called Gilli: "But many call to mind the man if they hear my nickname—I am called Gilli the Russian."

Hoskuld said he had often heard talk of him, and that he held him to be the richest of men that had ever belonged to the guild of merchants.

Still Hoskuld spoke: "You must have things to sell such as we should wish to buy." Gilli asked what he and his companions wished to buy.

Hoskuld said he should like to buy some bonds-woman, "if you have one to sell."

Gilli answers: "There, you mean to give me trouble by this, in asking for things you don't expect me to have in stock; but it is not sure that follows."

Hoskuld then saw that right across the booth there was drawn a curtain; and Gilli then lifted the curtain, and Hoskuld saw that there were twelve women seated behind the curtain. So Gilli said that Hoskuld should come on and have a look, if he would care to buy any of these women. Hoskuld did so. They sat all together across the booth. Hoskuld looks carefully at these women. He saw a woman sitting out by the skirt of the tent, and she was very ill-clad. Hoskuld thought, as far as he could see, this woman was fair to look upon.

Then said Hoskuld, "What is the price of that woman if I should wish to buy her?"

Gilli replied, "Three silver pieces is what you must weigh me out for her."

"It seems to me," said Hoskuld, "That you charge very highly for this bonds-woman, for that is the price of three (such)."

Then Gilli said, "You speak truly, that I value her worth more than the others. Choose any of the other eleven, and pay one mark of silver for her, this one being left in my possession."

Hoskuld said, "I must first see how much silver there is in the purse I have on my belt," and he asked Gilli to take the scales while he searched the purse.

Gilli then said, "On my side there shall be no guile in this matter; for, as to the ways of this woman, there is a great drawback which I wish, Hoskuld, that you know before we strike this bargain."

Hoskuld asked what it was.

Gilli replied, "The woman is dumb. I have tried in many ways to get her to talk, but have never got a word out of her, and I feel quite sure that this woman knows not how to speak."

Then, said Hoskuld, "Bring out the scales, and let us see how much the purse I have got here may weigh."

Gilli did so, and now they weigh the silver, and there were just three marks weighed.

Then said Hoskuld, "Now the matter stands so that we can close our bargain. You take the money for yourself, and I will take the woman. I take it that you have behaved honestly in this affair, for, to be sure, you had no mind to deceive me herein."

Hoskuld then went home to his booth. That same night Hoskuld went into bed with her.

The next morning when men got dressed, spake Hoskuld, "The clothes Gilli the Rich gave you do not appear to be very grand, though it is true that to him it is more of a task to dress twelve women than it is to me to dress only one."

After that Hoskuld opened a chest, and took out some fine women's clothes and gave them to her; and it was the saying of every one that she looked very well when she was dressed. But when the rulers had there talked matters over according as the law provided, this meeting was broken up. Then Hoskuld went to see King Hakon, and greeted him worthily, according to custom.

The king cast a side glance at him, and said, "We should have taken well your greeting, Hoskuld, even if you had saluted us sooner; but so shall it be even now."

Chapter XIII

Hoskuld Returns to Iceland, A.D. 948

After that the king received Hoskuld most graciously, and bade him come on board his own ship, and "be with us so long as you care to remain in Norway."

Hoskuld answered: "Thank you for your offer; but now, this summer, I have much to be busy about, and that is mostly the reason I was so long before I came to see you, for I wanted to get for myself house-timber."

The king bade him bring his ship in to the Wick, and Hoskuld tarried with the king for a while. The king got house-timber for him, and had his ship laden for him.

Then the king said to Hoskuld, "You shall not be delayed here longer than you like, though we shall find it difficult to find a man to take your place."

After that the king saw Hoskuld off to his ship, and said: "I have found you an honourable man, and now my mind misgives me that you are sailing for the last time from Norway, whilst I am lord over that land."

The king drew a gold ring off his arm that weighed a mark, and gave it to Hoskuld; and he gave him for another gift a sword on which there was half a mark of gold. Hoskuld thanked the king for his gifts, and for all the honour he had done him. After that Hoskuld went on board his ship, and put to sea. They had a fair wind, and hove in to the south of Iceland; and after that sailed west by Reekness, and so by Snowfellness in to Broadfirth. Hoskuld landed at Salmon-river-Mouth. He had the cargo taken out of his ship, which he took into the river and beached, having a shed built for it.

A ruin is to be seen now where he built the shed. There he set up his booths, and that place is called Booths'-Dale. After that Hoskuld had the timber taken home, which was very easy, as it was not far off. Hoskuld rode home after that with a few men, and was warmly greeted, as was to be looked for. He found that all his belongings had been kept well since he left.

Jorunn asked, "What woman that was who journeyed with him?"

Hoskuld answered, "You will think I am giving you a mocking answer when I tell you that I do not know her name."

Jorunn said, "One of two things there must be: either the talk is a lie that has come to my ears, or you must have spoken to her so much as to have asked her her name."

Hoskuld said he could not gainsay that, and so told her the truth, and bade that the woman should be kindly treated, and said it was his wish she should stay in service with them.

Jorunn said, "I am not going to wrangle with the mistress you have brought out of Norway, should she find living near me no pleasure; least of all should I think of it if she is both deaf and dumb."

Hoskuld slept with his wife every night after he came home, and had very little to say to the mistress. Every one clearly saw that there was something betokening high birth in the way she bore herself, and that she was no fool. Towards the end of the winter Hoskuld's mistress gave birth to a male child. Hoskuld was called, and was shown the child, and he thought, as others did, that he had never seen a goodlier or a more noble-looking child. Hoskuld was asked what the boy should be called. He said it should be named Olaf, for Olaf Feilan had died a little time before, who was his mother's brother. Olaf was far before other children, and Hoskuld bestowed great love on the boy.

The next summer Jorunn said, "That the woman must do some work or other, or else go away."

Hoskuld said she should wait on him and his wife, and take care of her boy besides. When the boy was two years old he had got full speech, and ran about like children of four years old. Early one morning, as Hoskuld had gone out to look about his manor, the weather being fine, and the sun, as yet little risen in the sky, shining brightly, it happened that he heard some voices of people talking; so he went down to where a little brook ran past the home-field slope, and he saw two people there whom he recognised as his son Olaf and his mother, and he discovered she was not speechless, for she was talking a great deal to the boy. Then Hoskuld went to her and asked her her name, and said it was useless for her to hide it any longer. She said so it should be, and they sat down on the brink of the field.

Then she said, "If you want to know my name, I am called Melkorka."

Hoskuld bade her tell him more of her kindred.

She answered, "Myr Kjartan is the name of my father, and he is a king in Ireland; and I was taken a prisoner of war from there when I was fifteen winters old."

Hoskuld said she had kept silence far too long about so noble a descent. After that Hoskuld went on, and told Jorunn what he had just found out during his walk.

Jorunn said that she "could not tell if this were true," and said she had no fondness for any manner of wizards; and so the matter dropped.

Jorunn was no kinder to her than before, but Hoskuld had

somewhat more to say to her. A little while after this, when Jorunn was going to bed, Melkorka was undressing her, and put her shoes on the floor, when Jorunn took the stockings and smote her with them about the head. Melkorka got angry, and struck Jorunn on the nose with her fist, so that the blood flowed. Hoskuld came in and parted them. After that he let Melkorka go away, and got a dwelling ready for her up in Salmon-river-Dale, at the place that was afterwards called Melkorkastad, which is now waste land on the south of the Salmon river. Melkorka now set up household there, and Hoskuld had everything brought there that she needed; and Olaf, their son, went with her. It was soon seen that Olaf, as he grew up, was far superior to other men, both on account of his beauty and courtesy.

If you enjoyed this book, please consider leaving a review on Amazon and Goodreads. A long review is not needed, just by adding a short sentence or two helps other potential readers find this book.

BOOKS BY RACHEL TSOUMBAKOS

Historical Fiction/Fantasy
Ragnar and the Women Who Loved Him (Viking Secrets #0)
Vikings: The Truth about Lagertha and Ragnar (Viking Secrets #1)
Vikings: The Truth about Thora and Ragnar (Viking Secrets #2)
Vikings: The Trouble with Ubbe's Mother (Viking Secrets #3)
Vikings: The Truth about Aslaug and Ragnar (Viking Secrets #4)
The Unnamed Warrior (Valkyrie Secrets #1)
Curse of the Valkyries (Valkyrie Secrets #2)
The Breaker of Curses (Valkyrie Secrets #3)
The Lost Viking (short story set in the same universe of Viking Secrets and Valkyrie Secrets)

Paranormal
Emeline and the Mutants
The Ring of Lost Souls
Metanoia
Unremembered Things

Horror
Zombie Apocalypse Now!
Make sure you sign up for my newsletter to find out when the next book in this series is due for release. You can do so here: bit.ly/RachelNL

Printed in Poland
by Amazon Fulfillment
Poland Sp. z o.o., Wrocław
26 October 2022

6d925b27-e710-461a-acb5-c3c863aa6c03R01